C0-CFC-961

John Locke

Series Introduction

The *Major Conservative and Libertarian Thinkers* series aims to show that there is a rigorous, scholarly tradition of social and political thought that may be broadly described as 'conservative', 'libertarian' or some combination of the two. The series aims to show that conservatism is not simply a reaction against contemporary events, nor a privileging of intuitive thought over deductive reasoning; libertarianism is not simply an apology for unfettered capitalism or an attempt to justify a misguided atomistic concept of the individual. Rather, the thinkers in this series have developed coherent intellectual positions that are grounded in empirical reality and also founded upon serious philosophical reflection on the relationship between the individual and society, how the social institutions necessary for a free society are to be established and maintained, and the implications of the limits to human knowledge and certainty.

Each volume in the series presents a thinker's ideas in an accessible and cogent manner to provide an indispensable work for both students with varying degrees of familiarity with the topic as well as more advanced scholars.

The following twenty volumes that make up the entire *Major Conservative and Libertarian Thinkers* series are written by international scholars and experts.

The Salamanca School by Andre Azevedo Alves (LSE, UK) &
 Professor José Manuel Moreira (Porto, Portugal)
Thomas Hobbes by Dr R. E. R. Bunce (Cambridge, UK)
John Locke by Professor Eric Mack (Tulane, US)
David Hume by Professor Christopher J. Berry (Glasgow, UK)
Adam Smith by Professor James Otteson (Yeshiva, US)
Edmund Burke by Professor Dennis O'Keeffe (Buckingham, UK)
Alexis de Tocqueville by Dr Alan S Kahan (Paris, France)
Herbert Spencer by Alberto Mingardi (Istituto Bruno Leoni, Italy)
Ludwig von Mises by Richard Ebeling (Trinity College)
Joseph A. Schumpeter by Professor John Medearis (Riverside, California, US)
F. A. Hayek by Dr Adam Tebble (UCL, UK)
Michael Oakeshott by Dr Edmund Neill (Oxford, UK)
Karl Popper by Dr Phil Parvin (Cambridge, UK)
Ayn Rand by Professor Mimi Gladstein (Texas, US)
Milton Friedman by Dr William Ruger (Texas State, US)
James M. Buchanan by Dr John Meadowcroft (King's College London, UK)
The Modern Papacy by Dr Samuel Gregg (Acton Institute, US)
Robert Nozick by Ralf Bader (St Andrews, UK)
Russell Kirk by Jon Pafford
Murray Rothbard by Gerard Casey

Of course, in any series of this nature, choices have to be made as to which thinkers to include and which to leave out. Two of the thinkers in the series – F. A. Hayek and James M. Buchanan – have written explicit statements rejecting the label 'conservative'. Similarly, other thinkers, such as David Hume and Karl Popper, may be more accurately described as classical liberals than either conservatives or libertarians. But these thinkers have been included because a full appreciation of this particular tradition of thought would be impossible without their inclusion; conservative and libertarian thought cannot be fully understood without some knowledge of the intellectual contributions of Hume, Hayek, Popper and Buchanan, among others. While no list of conservative and libertarian thinkers can be perfect, then, it is hoped that the volumes in this series come as close as possible to providing a comprehensive account of the key contributors to this particular tradition.

John Meadowcroft
King's College London

John Locke

Eric Mack

Major Conservative and
Libertarian Thinkers

Series Editor: John Meadowcroft

Volume 2

BLOOMSBURY

NEW YORK · LONDON · NEW DELHI · SYDNEY

Bloomsbury Academic

An imprint of Bloomsbury Publishing Plc

175 Fifth Avenue   50 Bedford Square

New York   London

NY 10010   WC1B 3DP

USA   UK

www.bloomsbury.com

Hardback edition first published in 2009 by the Continuum International Publishing Group Inc.
This paperback edition published by Bloomsbury Academic 2013

© Eric Mack, 2013

All rights reserved. No part of this publication may be reproduced or transmitted in any form or by any means, electronic or mechanical, including photocopying, recording, or any information storage or retrieval system, without prior permission in writing from the publishers.

No responsibility for loss caused to any individual or organization acting on or refraining from action as a result of the material in this publication can be accepted by Bloomsbury Academic or the author.

Library of Congress Cataloging-in-Publication Data
A catalog record for this book is available from the Library of Congress.

ISBN: HB: 978-0-8264-2981-0
PB: 978-1-4411-2322-0

Typeset by Deanta Global Publishing Services, Chennai, India
Printed and bound in the United States of America

Contents

Series Editor's Preface

John Locke was one of the great philosophers. His work offers enduring and important insights across a wide range of subjects, though he is probably best known for his contributions to political thought. At the heart of Locke's political philosophy is the belief that each individual possesses the right to life, liberty and property, and that these rights define the boundaries of a domain within which each individual may do as he or she wishes. For Locke, these are natural, or state of nature, rights that exist independent of any social contract or governmental authority.

Although Locke believed that the state of nature produced inconveniences which would lead men to enter into a commonwealth, Locke was nevertheless conscious of the possibility that those imbued with political authority may not respect their subjects' rights and in such a situation the concentration of power in the state would lead to violence and chaos rather than peace and order. Hence, for Locke, entering into political society did not involve giving up one's natural rights, but rather transferring to governmental authority the job of protecting those rights. If government failed to perform this function, or transgressed people's natural rights, then people were entitled to resist it, with force if necessary.

In this outstanding book Professor Eric Mack of Tulane University sets out Locke's philosophical position, places it in the context of the tumultuous political and religious events of seventeenth-century England, and subjects it to rigorous critical analysis. Mack argues that Locke provides an impressive, if not decisive, philosophical case for the view that individuals have natural rights to life, liberty and property, irrespective of the existence or actions of any political authority.

This volume makes a crucial contribution to the *Major Conservative and Libertarian Thinkers* series by setting out the thought of one of the most important contributors to this tradition. Certainly no account of libertarian or classical liberal thought would be complete without a thorough treatment of the contribution made by Locke. In presenting Locke's ideas in such an accessible and cogent form the author has produced an outstanding volume that will prove indispensable to those relatively unfamiliar with Locke's work as well as more advanced scholars.

John Meadowcroft
King's College London

Acknowledgments

By far my major institutional debt is to Liberty Fund, Inc. Through Liberty Fund's auspices I have been able to organize or attend intellectually stimulating colloquia on important figures in seventeenth-century political thought – including Robert Filmer, Thomas Hobbes, the Levellers, John Locke, and Pierre Bayle. In addition, I had the great good fortune to be a Resident Scholar at Liberty Fund during the spring of 2008 when this book was written. I also thank the Murphy Institute of Political Economy at Tulane University for a 2007 summer research grant that allowed me to begin to organize my thoughts on Locke. That process was also assisted by my department permitting me to teach several courses in seventeenth-century political philosophy over the past few years. I thank Jerry Gaus and Robert Berman for lively discussions about Hobbes and Locke, Sarah Skwire for encouraging my increasing fascination with the seventeenth century, and Hans Eicholz for helpful discussion about the influence of Locke. Mary has helped in more ways than I would have thought possible and, of course, this book is dedicated to her.

Eric Mack
Tulane University

Part 1

Intellectual Biography

1

The Historical and Ideological Context of Locke's Political Philosophy

John Locke is one of the great figures in the history of Western philosophy. He is one of the dozen or so thinkers who are remembered for their influential contributions across a broad spectrum of philosophical subfields—in Locke's case, across epistemology, the philosophy of language, the philosophy of mind, metaphysics, rational theology, ethics, and political philosophy. He was a seminal figure in the rise of the modern intellectual world. Today Locke is primarily remembered as a defender of empiricism in epistemology and of individualist liberalism in political theory. This work aims to present a systematic account of John Locke's political philosophy. This chapter lays out the main elements of that philosophy and the structure of the account that will follow; it also provides a brief sketch of the historical and ideological context of Locke's political thinking.

The Aims of This Work

To establish a point of departure and to define the task of this work, I shall start by stating certain fundamental tenets of political philosophy that are commonly and correctly understood to have been advanced by John Locke.

> Each individual possesses natural rights of life, liberty, and property; for each individual, these rights define the boundaries of a domain within which that individual may do as he sees fit.
> The rights of property, that is, individuals' rights to the fruits of their labor and to what they acquire in exchange for the fruits of their labor, flow from each individual's right over himself and his labor.

> The legitimate function of government is the articulation and
> protection of the rights of individuals to life, liberty, and property.
> Government derives its limited authority from the consent of the
> governed.
> Political rulers who infringe upon or even systematically fail to protect
> individual rights may rightfully be resisted and replaced.
> Political authority does not extend to the saving of men's souls.
> Respect for the rights of each individual and the voluntary asso-
> ciations individuals may form requires broad religious toleration.

The pivotal idea is that persons possess natural rights. To assert this is not
to say that persons are protected by some strange metaphysical shell.
Rather, it is to assert that certain fundamental facts about each person
provide *reasons* for others to be circumspect in their treatment of that
person, for example, reasons to avoid treating that person as material
which exists for their own use and purposes.[1]

The classical liberalism tradition in political thought takes the
primary, if not sole, political norm to be a prohibition on infringements
upon individual liberty. Liberty encompasses both the "personal" liberty
of, for example, choosing what religion one will practice and the
"economic" liberty of, for example, choosing which crop one will plant
in one's fields. The primary, if not sole, role of the government is the
protection of individuals' liberty. Thus, at least as a first approximation,
governments may employ force or the threat of force for the purpose of
defending individuals' liberty and only for this purpose. The radical limitation on the role of government is a boon rather than a hindrance to
mutually beneficial social order. For, within a framework of protected
individual liberty, persons voluntarily create and participate in a rich
variety of mutually advantageous economic and social relationships.
If my reading of Locke is correct, he stands as the historically most salient
expositor of a *rights-oriented* classical liberalism because his case for
liberty and its protection by a narrowly circumscribed government and
for resistance against tyrannical government is propelled by his contentions about rights.

My working hypothesis in this work is that Locke provides an impressive, if not decisive, philosophical case for the key tenets cited above—
except, for his doctrine of consent. I will document Locke's subscription
to these core tenets, identify the key philosophical arguments that Locke
offers for them, and display the persuasive force of Locke's arguments.

Fortunately, space does not permit me to enter expressly into the many deep scholarly controversies about how to interpret Locke's writings in political philosophy. While I do not think that everything Locke says relevant to political philosophy can be fit into the representation of Locke's position that I develop, I believe that more of what Locke says—especially more of what is really central to Locke's distinctive vision—cannot be fit into alternative interpretations of Locke.

Locke's best known work in political philosophy—the very core of Lockean political philosophy—is the *Second Treatise of Government*, which is Book II of Locke's *Two Treatises of Government*.[2] The *Second Treatise* takes us through the following key topics: the state of nature in which men are naturally equal and free; the law of nature which governs men in the state of nature; property rights; the introduction of money and the development of commercial society; the inconveniences of the state of nature and the need for and purpose of government; the origin of legitimate government in the consent of the governed; and the legitimacy of resistance to government which acts contrary to or fails to serve its specific purpose. The four chapters that follow this introduction track the logical arrangement of topics that Locke provides for us in the *Second Treatise*. The second chapter of this work deals with Locke's understanding of the state of nature and the law of nature that governs that state. The third chapter provides an account of Locke's doctrine of property rights, certain restrictions that apply to those rights, the invention of money, and the rise of commercial society. The fourth chapter concerns the inconveniences that beset the state of nature, the purpose of political authority, and the manner in which consent is supposed to give rise to political society and government. The fifth chapter deals largely with the grounds for resistance when those with political power either violate or fail to carry out their authorized purpose. The sixth chapter of this work examines Locke's important arguments in defense of religious toleration. These arguments are primarily advanced in the second most read of Locke's works within political philosophy—his *A Letter Concerning Toleration* (1983). As we shall see, the arguments of the *Second Treatise* and of the *Letter* are intricately intertwined and mutually supportive. All of the five central chapters will draw upon additional material from Locke's body of political writings. Chapter 7 discusses the reception of Locke's political thought in the several generations after his death and then returns to central themes in Locke's political theory which are of current philosophical relevance.

A Century of Ideological and Political Conflict

To set the stage for Locke's political philosophy and for brief accounts of the views of his two main authoritarian opponents, Robert Filmer and Thomas Hobbes, we need a quick background sketch of the politically turbulent century in which these men lived and wrote. James I, son of Mary Queen of Scots and previously James VI of Scotland, ascended to the English throne in 1603. At least from the time of James' ascension through the Glorious Revolution of 1688, England was riven by a set of interconnected conflicts concerning the proper extent and location of religious and political authority.[3]

At the center of the religious dimension of this conflict was the Anglican Church with its rigid hierarchy and its high church tone; the Church of England was, of course, officially presided over by the king and its hierarchy was closely allied to the English monarch. From the right (so to speak) the Anglican Church was threatened by plots to bring England back to Catholicism by force of arms and by the peaceful succession to the throne of either a Catholic sympathizer or convert. From the left (so to speak) the established Anglican Church was under attack from Puritanism with its demands for a less ritualized, less Popish, more Scripturally oriented, and locally governed churches and, from further yet on the left, more radically dissenting Protestant groups. Numerous writers argued that social and political peace required that some specific brand of Christianity be enforced throughout the land. On the other hand, at least from the 1640s and onward, many other authors defended a regime of religious toleration. There was conflict over which religion should be imposed and also conflict over whether any (specific) religion should be imposed. Along the dimension of political authority, the seventeenth-century dispute was similarly twofold. First, which political body, the monarch or the parliament ought to rule? Or, if not one or the other alone, what should be the division of political authority between the monarch and the parliament? Second, wherever political authority should be lodged, how extensive should that authority be? Is political authority, wherever it is best placed, unlimited—so that, for example, it may be used to require everyone to practice the one established religion? Or is political authority, wherever it is best placed, itself subject to lawful constraints?

So, in religion, we have pro-Catholic factions, pro-Anglican factions, pro-Puritan factions, pro-dissenter factions and cutting across these divisions anti-tolerance and pro-tolerance factions. In politics, we have pro-monarchial factions and pro-parliamentary factions and cutting across these divisions advocates of unlimited authority and advocates of constrained authority. Add in all the more parochial and less ideological bases for the loyalties and animosities which people form and one has a recipe for endlessly shifting alliances and endlessly changing points of conflict. Nevertheless, alliances of sufficient duration formed in the 1640s for the English to fight a civil war that ended in the execution of Charles I in 1649 and to conduct a revolution in 1688 which ousted James II and brought the invading William of Orange to the throne (along with his wife, Mary).

Although James I was an explicit advocate of absolute monarchical authority, he was a much more subtle politician than his son, Charles, who succeeded him in 1625. Charles I was almost continually embroiled in conflicts with his subjects over religion, taxation, and the prerogatives of Parliament. Civil war broke out in 1642 between opponents and supporters of the monarchical political and ecclesiastical authority. All efforts at comprise between the stubborn and pompous Charles and the increasing radical anti-monarchical coalition failed. Finally the captured (and recaptured) Charles was tried and convicted of treason in January 1649. The monarchy and the House of Lords were abolished. Oliver Cromwell, who had risen to be the dominant military leader in the struggle against Charles I, ruled as Lord Protector of the Commonwealth from 1653 until his death in 1658. A new Parliament—including a revivified House of Lords—met in 1660 and invited Charles I's son to return as king. From the time of Charles II's return in 1661, the same complex of conflicts that seemingly had culminated in the Charles I's execution began to be replayed. Correctly or not, Charles II's willingness to extend toleration to Catholics was seen as part of a move to reestablish a highly authoritarian political and religious order. By the mid-1670s two political coalitions had formed—a *Whig* coalition favoring limits on monarchial power and at least some degree of toleration for dissenting religious persuasions and a *Tory* coalition favoring discretionary monarchical power and the domination of religious life by the Church of England (or perhaps even the Church of Rome).

The chief leader of the Whig camp was the Earl of Shaftsbury; and the chief cause of the Whigs by the late 1670s was the passage of an Exclusion Act that would preclude any Catholic from becoming the English monarch. Charles II was (rightly) suspected of having Catholic inclinations and intentions and, more worrisome yet, his heir—Charles' younger brother James—had converted to Catholicism in 1673. Exclusion Bills were passed in the House of Commons in 1679 and 1680, but neither were approved by the House of Lords. In 1681 Charles dissolved Parliament before the Commons could once again move for Exclusion. Shaftsbury was charged with treason; but the charge was invalidated by a sympathetic London grand jury. Shaftsbury attempted unsuccessfully to rally his supporters to insurrection against Charles. When that effort failed, he fled to Holland in November 1682, where he died in January 1683. Later in 1683 radical remnants of Shaftsbury's Whig followers were arrested, tried, and executed for their participation in the Rye House plot to assassinate Charles and James. Charles II died in1685 and was succeeded by the Catholic James. The birth of a son to James II in June of 1688 who would be raised as a Catholic heir to the throne forged an alliance of Whig and Tory noblemen to urge William of Orange (whose wife, Mary, was James II' Protestant daughter) to rescue England from popery and arbitrary power. William landed with his army in November of 1688, much of the country rallied to William, and James fled to France. The Bill of Rights that followed placed limits upon monarchial power and reasserted what were taken to be the traditional rights of Parliament and of individuals. A moderate degree of religious toleration—less than hoped for by the main advocates of toleration—was enacted.

It was into this era of conflict that John Locke was born in Somerset county in southwest England in 1632. His father, John Locke, was a not very successful lawyer who served as clerk for the Justices of the Peace in Somerset and also as the personal attorney for one of the Justices, Alexander Popham. Early in the civil war, Popham organized and lead a troop of Parliamentary soldiers; and John Locke, the father, served as a captain in that troop. Through the good offices of Popham, John Locke, the son, was admitted to the prestigious Westminster School in 1647. Locke moved on to Christ Church at Oxford in 1652. Locke was dissatisfied with the education offered at Oxford, which was still classical in content and scholastic in form. He increasingly associated himself with a circle of experimental scientists in Oxford, the most prominent of whom was Robert Boyle. Locke turned especially to the empirical study of medicine. Locke's decision not to seek ordination made him ineligible for most of the senior studentships at Christ Church. However, in 1675— after he had substantially moved on to non-academic pastures—Locke was appointed to one of the two studentships in medicine. During the late 1650s and early 1660s Locke shared the fatigue that the nation as a whole felt from many years of political disorder and uncertainty. In 1660–1661 Locke composed, but did not publish, two essays—now known as the "Two Tracts on Government" (Locke 1997, pp.3–78)—which expressed strongly authoritarian views with respect to the sovereign's authority over religious matters. He disdained the enthusiasm of deviant Protestant sects and he welcomed the Restoration of the Stuarts. In 1663–1664, he delivered a series of lectures at his college—now known as the *Essays on the Law of Nature* (1997, pp.79–133)—in which Locke first defends his epistemological claims that all of human knowledge ultimate derives from sense experience, and no knowledge comes in the form of "innate ideas."

The pivotal moment in Locke's life was his meeting the Earl of Shaftsbury—at that point, still Lord Ashley—in Oxford in 1666. Within a year Locke joined the Whig leader's household in London as his personal physician and as an important member of Shaftsbury's brain trust. Locke's entrance into Shaftsbury's circle was accompanied by a very marked transformation of Locke's political views. For in 1667 he composed, but did not publish, what is now known as "An Essay on Toleration" (1997, pp.134–59) which foreshadowed both his later defenses of religious toleration and his later liberal account of the purpose of government. In 1668 Locke solidified his relationship with Shaftsbury by supervising a lifesaving operation which inserted a duct to drain an abscess in Shaftsbury liver.

In London, Locke continued his pursuit of experimental science and empirical medical studies. Conversations with friends on religious and moral topics convinced him that the first intellectual necessity was an account of the nature and limits of human knowledge. In 1671 he composed the first draft of what was to become the *Essay Concerning Human Understanding*. In the later 1670s, Locke lived in France meeting with French scientists and anti-Cartesian philosophers and, perhaps, gathering intelligence for Shaftsbury about negotiations between the King of France and Charles II. Locke returned to London in 1679 and rejoined Shaftsbury who had been released from a year's imprisonment in the Tower of London. Over the next couple of years, the fight over an Exclusion Bill raged. During the Exclusion crisis supporters of monarchical authority resurrected the writings of Robert Filmer. Locke almost certainly wrote the basic text of the *Two Treatises of Government*, the first book of which is entirely devoted to an attack on Filmer's patriarchalism, during the Exclusion crisis or the succeeding year or so when Shaftsbury and his allies were attempting to organize an insurrection against Charles. After Shaftsbury fled to Holland, radical Whig attempts to unseat Charles and block the ascendance of James continued, largely in the form of the abortive Rye House plot. Within a couple of days of that plot being betrayed—and before its betrayal was publicly known—Locke left London to settle his affairs in Oxford and Somerset; and then he too fled to Holland. There is good evidence, albeit no one smoking musket, that while he remained in England Locke was deeply involved in the conspiracies against Charles and that, while he was in Holland, he was deeply involved in attempts to launch further insurrections against Charles and then James.[4] This was certainly the view of Charles II when he ordered the obedient officials of Christ Church to strip Locke of his studentship in late 1684.

While he hid out in Holland, Locke continued to work on his *Essay Concerning Human Understanding* (*ECHU*); it was published in December of 1689. Locke also composed his *Epistola de Tolerantia* which was published in May of 1689 and in English translation, as *A Letter Concerning Toleration*, in October 1689. Almost simultaneously, Locke published his *Two Treatises of Government*, minus the large portion of the *First Treatise* against Filmer that had been lost or destroyed while Locke was in exile. The *ECHU* was the only one of these writings to which Locke attached his name, and it quickly established Locke as a major philosophical figure. After his return to England in February 1690, following the Glorious Revolution of 1688, Locke served on a variety of governmental commissions. Among his important further publications were *A Second Letter Concerning Toleration* in 1690, *A Third Letter for Toleration* in 1692, and *The Reasonableness of Christianity* in 1695. Locke died in 1704.

The Political Authoritarianism of Robert Filmer

Seventeenth-century England witnessed an incredible outpouring of political theorizing. Among the doctrines presented were two apparently quite different defenses of the authoritarian view that political authority—political sovereignty—is and ought to be unlimited and undivided. These were the doctrines of Robert Filmer (1588–1653) and Thomas Hobbes (1588–1679). Both were inspired by the political and ideological disorder that lead to and fully manifested itself in the English Civil War.

I can provide here only highly simplified statements of the key contentions of Filmer and of Hobbes. Nevertheless, I believe these statements
capture the basic picture that Locke had of his intellectual opponents.
Filmer's work, *Patriarcha: The Natural Power of Kinges Defended against the
Unnatural Liberty of the People*, (1991, pp.1–68) was probably composed in
the 1630s or early 1640s, and some of the material from it appeared in
political tracts which Filmer published in the late 1640s and early 1650s.
But *Patriarcha* itself was first published in 1680—almost three decades
after Filmer's death and at the height of the Exclusion controversy when,
once again, there was a powerful confrontation between friends and foes
of unlimited monarchical power. *Patriarcha* became one of, if not the
most, prominent intellectual defense of the ultimate and absolute legal
authority of the monarch. Filmer is known to us today almost entirely
because Locke and other foes of unlimited monarchical authority[5] felt
the need to compose refutations of him. *Patriarcha* is a vehement attack
on the following train of reasoning: Men are naturally equal and free;
political authority is established through the consent of such equal and
free individuals; through their consent individuals create a limited political authority; political authority may overstep its rightful bounds, and
when it does, it may be lawfully resisted.

Filmer believed that he could derail this train of reasoning at the start
by pointing out that no man (since Adam) has been born free; every
man is born subject to the authority of his father. The relevance of this
to *political* authority is simple; political authority is nothing but paternal
authority. For Filmer, this is not intended as a metaphor. Political authority began with Adam's absolute fatherly authority over his children (and
also his authority over Eve). Indeed, it was perfectly within Adams'
authority to kill any of his children if he chose to do so (Filmer 1991,
p.7). Moreover, Adam's absolute authority extended to all the descendents of his children. Adam was the first father, the first patriarch, and
the first monarch all rolled into one. Filmer also held that God had
donated all of the earth and all of its creatures to Adam. Hence, Adam
began as the supreme father *and* the supreme proprietor. At Adams'
death, his unlimited and undivided paternal authority was inherited in
full by his eldest (surviving) son. Similarly, at that eldest son's death, *his*
eldest son inherited in full all of the paternal authority that Adam would
have were Adam still alive. And so on. The absolute authority of current
rulers is their inheritance from Adam's original and natural authority.
Filmer's claims, strange as they may sound to us today, resonated deeply

with the patriarchal character and self-understanding of seventeenth-century society and with the long tradition of thinking of kings as being fathers to their subjects.

On Filmer's theory it is hard to see how at any given moment there could be more than one rightful ruler on earth. To deal with this problem, Filmer mentions a couple of occasions on which paternal/political authority has fragmented. After the Flood and Noah's death, each of his three sons (and also, somehow, some of his nephews!) became father to and king of his own people. The confusion at the tower of Babel fragmented mankind into 72 nations—albeit all of these nations "were distinct families that had fathers for rulers over them" (1991, pp.7–8). Indeed, Filmer makes further rather desperate moves to bring his theory into line with his ambition of vindicating the authority of *existing* monarchs. In his most desperate moment, Filmer tells us that,

> It skills [i.e., matters] not which way kings come by their power, whether by election, donation, succession or by any other means, for it is still the manner of the government by supreme power that makes them properly kings, and not the means of obtaining their crowns. (Filmer 1991, p.44)

Yet now it seems that the pedigree of a ruler as an heir of Adam matters not at all; all that matters for a ruler to be "properly" a king is that he have supreme, that is, unlimited and unshared, power. Thus, in his attempt to accommodate the legitimacy of all existing political power, Filmer seems to abandon his distinctively patriarchal doctrine. So much for Filmer's positive patriarchal view.

Yet there is a lot more to Filmer than the doctrine which has been his claim to infamy. Three other features of Filmer's views need to be appreciated: his negative case against natural equality and liberty and the consensual grounding of political authority; his powerful advocacy of what I will call "legal voluntarism"; and his contention that people are likely to be better off under unlimited monarchical power than under popular governance.

Filmer makes two very interesting and parallel arguments against men's natural equality and freedom. According to the first argument, the hypothesis that men are naturally equal and free leads to the absurd consequence that no government has ever or ever will be legitimate. For, if men are naturally equal and free, then unanimous consent is necessary in order for legitimate political power to exist. Yet unanimous consent has never and will never occur. Hence, if men are naturally equal and free, there has never been and there will never be legitimate political power. Since this is an absurd conclusion, the premise that yields it, viz., that men are naturally equal and free, must be false. According to the second argument, the hypothesis that men are naturally equal and free leads to the absurd consequence that no private property has ever or will ever be legitimate. For, if men are naturally equal and free, then the earth is initially commonly owned and unanimous consent is necessary for any part of the earth to become anyone's legitimate private property. Yet unanimous consent to create private property has never and will never occur. Hence, if men are naturally equal and free, there has never been and there will never be legitimate private property. Since this is an absurd conclusion, the premise that yields it, viz., that men are naturally equal and free, must be false (1991, p.234).

Second, Filmer was a bold advocate of legal voluntarism. By "legal voluntarism" I mean the view that whatever the earthly sovereign wills is the law and only what the earthly sovereign wills is law. Whoever the sovereign is—an individual or an assembly or even the people as a whole—his or its *will* constitutes the law. Since the sovereign's will is the source of the law, the sovereign himself cannot be subject to the law. Filmer defends this voluntarism most powerfully, in *The Anarchy of a Limited or Mixed Monarchy* (1991, pp.131–71). Filmer begins by directly confronting the common maxim that society should be governed by law and not arbitrary power.

> We do but flatter ourselves, if we hope ever to be governed without an arbitrary power. No, we mistake. The question is not, whether there shall be an arbitrary power, but the only point is who shall have that arbitrary power, whether one man or many? There never was nor ever can be any people governed without a power of making laws, and every power of making laws must be arbitrary. For to make a law according to law, is *contradicto in adjecto* [self-contradictory]. (1991, p.132)

What does Filmer mean when he says that to make a law according to law is self-contradictory? Why can't a body of higher law, for example, constitutional law, set limits for ordinary statutory law? Filmer's answer relies upon his premise that a (self-conscious, willful) law maker is prior to the law. Suppose there were a higher-order constitutional law that controlled the generation of statutory law. It itself would have to exist as the expressed will of some other (earthly) agent; and that higher agent's commands will have legal force only through that agent's power to punish violators of his will. Thus, the apparent governance of statutory law by some higher order law would really be its governance by *the arbitrary, uncontrolled will* of that higher agent. That higher agent over whom there is no law would be the real (earthly) sovereign. Whoever he is, the sovereign comes first; and from the sovereign comes his instrument, the law. Note that Filmer's argument for the legal supremacy of the sovereign's will is quite independent of his patriarchal defense of monarchial power—or of any preference that he has for monarchical rule.

As one would expect, however, Filmer's view is that legally unconstrained monarchical rule was far better than legally unconstrained popular rule. Tyrannical monarchs may indeed engage in "bloody acts." Nevertheless, "the cruelty of such tyrants extends ordinarily no further than to some particular men that offend them, and not to the whole kingdom" (1991, p.30). For monarchs have an eye to their own advantage and what is most to their advantage is that their subjects be secure in their lives and their possessions.

. . . if not out of affection to his people, yet out of natural love to himself, every tyrant desires to preserve the lives and protect the goods of his subjects, which cannot be done but by justice, and if it be not done, the prince's loss is the greatest. (1991, p.31)

In contrast, under popular government, no member of the assembly has much incentive to preserve the lives and protect the goods of members of the society. Hence, "everyone leaves the business for his fellow until it is quite neglected by all." Moreover, no member of the assembly need worry that his neglect of that business or even his contribution to the injury of others will bring retaliation against him. For "where wrong is done to any particular person by a multitude," the wronged individual "knows not who hurt him, or who to complain of, or to whom to address himself for reparation." In contrast, a monarch has to worry much more that he will be identified by those he victimizes and that "the meanest of his subjects . . . may find a means to revenge himself of the injustice that is offered him" (1991, p.31). So, beyond his patriarchalism, Filmer argues quite powerfully that political authority cannot be founded upon the consent of the governed, that political authority can never be legally constrained, and subjects are better off under absolute monarchical rule than they are under popular rule.

The Political Authoritarianism of Thomas Hobbes

Thomas Hobbes, who stands with Locke as one of the primary figures in the history of Western philosophy, also formulated his political views in response to the conflict which lead up to and culminated in the English Civil War. Between 1640 and 1650, he circulated and published *The Elements of Law* (1928) and *De cive* (*On the Citizen*) (1998). The doctrine expounded in these works was reformulated and refined in his masterwork, *Leviathan*, (1994) which Hobbes published in 1651. Hobbes begins with the premise which Filmer believes is manifestly false, viz., that men are naturally equal and free. For Hobbes rejects the premodern and Filmerite idea that there is a natural moral hierarchy among men. Indeed, according to Hobbes, not only is there no natural moral hierarchy among men (and, hence, no natural *political* authority); there is no natural moral order at all. Men are by nature masterless—both in the sense that there is no natural authority of one man over another and in the sense men are not naturally subject to any moral laws.[6] Therefore, in men's natural condition, nothing is morally forbidden, nothing is unlawful or unjust; everything is permissible.

Like Filmer, Hobbes embraces legal voluntarism. The only possible source of law—indeed, of any binding norms—is the will of the earthly sovereign. But, contrary to Filmer, no such sovereign exists by nature. Hence, in man's natural circumstances, no sovereign exists whose will can make certain conduct lawful and other conduct unlawful. Hobbes expresses the idea that nothing in the state of nature is forbidden or is unlawful, by saying that in the absence of political authority each man has a right to everything; each has a right to do anything. But we should not be mislead—and Hobbes is not mislead—by this talk of rights which exist in the state of nature. For each person's rights in the state of nature consist simply in that person not be subject to any normative constraints on his actions. Tom has a right to his body and to dispose of his body as he sees fit; but Tom also has a right to John's body and to dispose of John's body as he sees fit. For just as Tom has no natural obligation to submit to John's killing him, Tom has no natural obligation not to kill John. Similarly, just as John has no natural obligation to submit to Tom's killing him, John has no natural obligation not to kill Tom. To say that in the state of nature every man has the right to do everything is simply to say that the state of nature is a moral free-for-all. Moreover, in the absence of political authority, men *will* exercise their blameless liberties to kill, enslave, and maim one another. Human beings are always primarily motivated by the desire for self-preservation; albeit some of us are also moved by the desire for glory (1994, xiii, 4–7). In the state of nature, we each see predation upon others as a prospective means of advancing our ends or see preemptive attacks on others as necessary to protect ourselves from their predation. We each see each other as being disposed to predatory or preemptive attacks and that, in turn, heightens the *rationality* of each of us being moved toward killing, enslaving, and maiming others. Although each of us would do better to live at peace with our fellows, under the circumstances of the state of nature, we will be driven to ceaseless conflict.

> Hereby it is manifest that during the time men live without a common power to keep them all in awe, they are in that condition which is called war, and such a war as is of every man against every man. (1994, I, xiii, 8)

Perhaps the most famous passage from Hobbes is his description of consequences of the war of all against all.

> . . . there is no place for industry, because the fruit thereof is uncertain, and consequently, no culture of the earth, no navigation, nor use of the commodities that may be imported by sea, no commodious building, no instruments of moving and removing such things as require much force, no knowledge of the face of the earth, no account of time, no arts, no letters, no society, and which is worst of all, continual fear and danger of violent death, and the life of man, solitary, poor, nasty, brutish, and short. (1994, I, xiii, 9)

It is our *misfortune* that Filmer is mistaken in his belief that hierarchy and subordination are natural to us. We must, according to Hobbes, overcome this natural misfortune by substituting artificial inequality and authority for our natural equality and liberty. We must create an artificial earthly sovereign whose absolute authority will deliver us from the war of all upon all.

Hobbes describes two different ways by which such a sovereign can be created. Both seem to involve men's total surrender of their state of nature rights. The first way is "sovereignty by institution." Grasping the horrors of the war of all upon all and of the role that our unlimited rights play in the generation of that war, all of us but one mutually agree to surrender up these rights. This leaves the one party who has not surrendered his rights with the right to do anything whatsoever to us and to command anything of us; and it leaves us a duty not to resist that party's actions and to obey that party's commands (1994, I, xiv, 7). This party, therefore, becomes our earthly sovereign. He is an earthly sovereign who has no contractual duties to his subjects—because he has not entered into any compact with them. Nor does he have any natural duties to his subjects—for no natural duties exist. He is fully unbound in his treatment of his subjects as any individual is unbound toward others in the state of nature. Moreover, this sovereign's will is the law. As the source of the law, the sovereign himself cannot act unlawfully. Whatever the sovereign does, he wills to do; and if he wills to do it, it is for that reason lawful. For Hobbes, as for Filmer, there can be no laws that stand outside of the sovereign and govern how he may act. For, if there were any such law, it would have to proceed from some other agent's will and *that* agent would be the true sovereign. Hobbes' voluntarism takes a particularly extreme form because Hobbes also holds that justice is nothing but legality. Hence, anything the sovereign does or commands is just; there are no principles of justice which stand outside of the sovereign on the basis of which anything that the sovereign does or commands can be said to be unjust. Moreover, in practice the belief that subjects can appeal to the authority of independent norms of law or justice to contest the will of the sovereign is a recipe for civil war. Peace is the great value for Hobbes and, he thinks, any belief in limited or divided authority destroys peace.

There are, according to Hobbes, certain rules—which Hobbes *calls* "laws of nature"—general compliance with which is advantageous to all men, for example, the rules against killing, plundering, and contractual default. However, individuals will not abide by these rules in the state of nature because no man has assurance that others will reciprocate that compliance. When men contract together to institute a sovereign, they do so with the *hope* that the sovereign will command compliance with these rules. Such commands—backed by sufficiently terrorizing threats of punishment—will deliver his subjects from the state of war of all upon all.

Of course, the sovereign is primarily interested in his own self-preservation, not in the welfare of his subjects. But it is in the interest of the sovereign to reign over an internally peaceful and prosperous society. Hence, if he is sensible, he will create laws against, for example, murder, theft, and contractual default, which will engender peaceful coexistence and cooperation among his subjects. For, being in a state of war with all other sovereigns, this ruler needs a wealthy and populous society from which to draw cannons and cannon fodder.

The sovereign, however, cannot be bound by law or by justice to enact or abide by these "laws of nature." And any belief that the sovereign is so bound is a belief in a competing authority and so engenders civil war. To get a sovereign who can end the war of all upon all, aspiring subjects must take the plunge and create a ruler with unlimited and undivided authority. That ruler may turn out to be brutal and rapacious. But the worst that can happen under such a ruler

> . . . is scarce sensible, in respect of the miseries and horrible calamities that accompany a civil war (or that dissolute condition of masterless men, without subjection to laws and a coercive power to tie their hands from rapine and revenge) . . . (1994, II, xviii, 20)

When push comes to shove—and it always does for Hobbes—our choice is between civil or perpetual war and "arbitrary government" (1994, II, xlvi, 35).

There are two obvious problems with Hobbes' story about commonwealth by institution. First, it is hard to see how, within a state of war of all upon all, men could come together to engage in the mutual conditional divestiture of rights which Hobbes describes. Second, even if men did enter into such a covenant, according to Hobbes, it itself will have no binding force except if a power sufficient to keep them all in awe appears at the moment of the covenant. For ". . . the validity of covenants begins not but with the constitution of a civil power sufficient to compel men to keep them" (1994, II, xv, 3). Yet there is no reason to think that a pledge by these men to reciprocally divest themselves of their rights itself will bring into existence a common power which will make that pledge binding. So Hobbes, like Filmer, has to turn to the *true* story of the rise of sovereigns. In truth, sovereignty arises "by acquisition," that is, by conquest and by consent that is wrung out of the conquered. A conqueror—*any* conqueror—has both the power and the right (blameless liberty) to kill all those he has conquered. In return for their pledge of obedience, the conqueror simply stays his hand. Their pledge transforms the vanquished into subjects and the conqueror into their sovereign. That act of submission obligates the vanquished to obey the commands of the conqueror; but it cannot obligate the conqueror who has merely chosen for the moment not to exercise his right to kill the vanquished. The resulting unlimited authority of the sovereign is not the natural authority of the conqueror but, rather, it is an artifact of the consent of the conquered. That authority exists, according to Hobbes, "because [the vanquished] cometh in, and submitteth to the victor." (1994, II, xx, 11).

In a sense the ultimate problem in the state of nature is not men's natural equality and freedom but, rather, men's reliance on their own private judgments, their own private reason. If there were a common judge of how men should act to which all men would defer, their natural equality and freedom would not drive them into conflict. According to Hobbes, right reason is "the reason of some arbitrator or judge" to whom the contending parties must defer. Since there is no "right reason constituted by nature" and yet men need right reason as a common arbiter of how they shall act, right reason must be *created*. It is created with the creation of the sovereign. For right reason is "the reason [or, more accurately, the will] of this our artificial man, the commonwealth, and his command that maketh law" (1994, II, xxvi, 11). With the creation of a sovereign, mankind enters a state in which "Not the appetite of private men, but the law which is the will and appetite of the state, is the measure" (1994 II, xlvi, 32).[7] Filmer too it should be noted recoiled from the prospect of private judgment. For ". . . if any man may be judge what law is contrary to God's will, to nature, or to reason, it will soon bring in confusion" (1991, p.204).

The seventeenth century was a world awash with private judgment, that is, with more people in more ways thinking that it was appropriate—indeed, necessary—for them as individuals to exercise their own judgment and reason whether it be in matters of religion, of economic endeavor, or of politics. It was a world in which the static acceptance of tradition and authority was being everywhere challenged with the rise of the idea that people ought to judge for themselves, that autonomy in belief and action was an essential human value. Perhaps the most reactionary feature of Hobbes' worldview is his recoil against this tide of private judgment—a recoil based largely on the traditionalist belief that peace and order requires uniformity of belief and unity of purpose.

Part 2

Critical Exposition

2

Natural Freedom, Natural Law, and Natural Rights

Like Hobbes, Locke's political theorizing begins with the state of nature. The motivating idea of state of nature theorizing is that we can determine what the purpose and proper extent of political authority is by seeing what sort of problems would beset us in the absence of all political authority. For the purpose of political authority is simply to deal with the problems that would exist due to the absence of political governance. And the proper extent of political authority is the extent of authority that individuals in the state of nature establish to solve the problems that arise because of the absence of such governance. This is why, Locke stated: "To understand political power right, and derive it from its original, we must consider what state all men are naturally in" (1980, II, 4). For Hobbes, as we have seen, the problems of the state of nature are horrendous and deep-seated. They go at least as deep as moral anarchy, that is, the absence of any sound norms on the basis of which individuals might peacefully coexist. Hence, individuals need to create a political authority which itself generates the norms which govern men's conduct and, hence, is not itself subject to any constraining norms. For Locke, the problems of the state of nature are less horrendous and less deep-seated largely because the state of nature "has a law of nature to govern it" (1980, II, 6). The law of nature—at the core of which are men's rights over their own lives, liberties, and possessions—provides some basis for peaceful coexistence within the state of nature and a basis for men's establishment of political authority. Since, for Locke, political authority is created in order to better enforce this independently sound law of nature, political authority itself is not the source of the basic norms that govern men's conduct and, hence, political authority can and is bound by this law of nature. That is, it is constrained by persons' pre-political natural rights. Locke agrees with Hobbes that men are naturally equal and free; against Filmer, he agrees that there is no natural hierarchy among men and no natural political authority. But, against Hobbes, Locke maintains that there is a natural moral order—a moral order that is not created by the will of the sovereign. This order provides guidance to men in the state of nature, limits the authority of any government created by men, and ultimately provides the basis for resistance against governments that violate the limits of their created authority.

Locke reminds us of two main difficulties with Filmer's account of political authority. First, Locke's detailed critique of Filmer's arguments for patriarchalism reveals that

> . . . it is impossible that rulers now on earth should make any benefit, or derive any the least shadow of authority from that, which is held to be the fountain of all power, *Adam's private dominion and parental jurisdiction* . . . (1980, II, 1)

Second, Filmer himself abandons his patriarchal stance when he declares that "It skills not which way kings come by their power, whether it be election, donation, succession or by any other means" (1991, p.44). As Locke remarks in the *First Treatise* after he quotes this passage from Filmer,

> And he might have spared the trouble of speaking so much, as he does, up and down of Heirs and Inheritance, if to make any one *properly a King*, needs no more but *Governing by Supreme Power, and it matters not by what Means he came by it.* (1960, I, 78)

Unless we find "another rise of government, another original of political power," we will be forced to believe that, ". . . all government in the world is the product only of force and violence, and that men live together by no other rules but that of beasts, where the strongest carries it" (1980, II, 1). That is to say, we will be forced to adopt what Locke takes to be the upshot of Hobbes' doctrine. And this Hobbesian doctrine is self-defeating because in reality it "lay[s] a foundation for perpetual disorder and mischief, tumult, sedition and rebellion (things that the followers of that hypothesis so loudly cry out against) . . ." (1980, II, 1). This is because people will never accept the brute power of their ruler as basis for their subordination to that ruler; people will always resist power which has no moral basis. According to Locke, while Filmer's doctrine sows the seeds of conflict by making it impossible to figure out who the current true patriarch is (1960, I, 104–106), Hobbes' doctrine sows the seeds of conflict by telling people that there is no basis in morality or justice for political authority.

So we need to go back to the state of nature drawing board and especially investigate what basis there is for belief in a law of nature which governs the state of nature and what the content of that law of nature is. In the first section of this chapter, "Perfect Freedom" I begin that inquiry with Locke's "perfect freedom" argument for each individual's natural right to dispose of his person and actions as he sees it. This discussion will further contrast the Hobbesian and Lockean approaches and set the stage for the explication and assessment of four further arguments by Locke on behalf of natural rights. Unfortunately, a significant complication arises from the fact that Locke seems to offer two quite distinct and apparently incompatible doctrines concerning the law of nature. These are the "inborn constitution" program and "divine voluntarism" doctrine. In the second section, I pause to come to terms with the presence in Locke of both of these views. In sections three and four, I explicate and assess four further arguments provided by Locke for each individual's natural right to dispose of his actions and person (and his possessions) as he sees fit. The fifth section deals with the relationship between the pursuit of happiness and compliance with the laws of nature.

Perfect Freedom

A pivotal difference between Hobbes and Locke is conveyed in Locke's claim that the state of nature is

> . . . *a state of perfect freedom* to order their actions, and dispose of their possessions, and person, as they think fit, within the bounds of the law of nature, without asking leave or depending upon the will of any other man. (1980, II, 4)

Natural freedom consists in each person being free to order *his* actions and dispose of *his* possessions and person as he thinks fit. One's natural freedom does *not* include the freedom to order any other individual's action or possession or person as one sees fit. Indeed, the law of nature precludes one from ordering any other person's actions or disposing of any other person or any other person's possession—at least if one has not gotten the consent of that person to do so. Correlatively this law of nature precludes others from doing with one as they see fit.

Is it an imperfection of this natural freedom that it does not include
the freedom to do to others or their possessions whatever one sees fit to
do? Is the natural freedom that Hobbes affirms—which includes the
freedom to do anything to anybody—a more perfect freedom than the
natural freedom affirmed by Locke? Locke's answer is that "freedom is
not as we are told [by, e.g., Hobbes] *a liberty for every man to do what he lists;*
(for who could be free, when every other man's humour might domi-
neer over him?) . . . ." A freedom which is accompanied by others being
entirely free to intrude upon and destroy one is, Locke contends, a radically imperfect freedom. The more perfect liberty is

. . . a *liberty* to dispose, and order, as he lists, his person, actions,
possessions, and his whole property within the allowance of those laws
under which he is; and therein not to be subject to the arbitrary will of
another, but freely follow his own.

Therefore, perfect liberty requires law that precludes all individuals
from disposing of others or their possessions. "For *liberty* is to be free
from restraint and violence from others which cannot be, where there is
no law . . ." (1980, II, 57). In the state of nature especially, the law in
virtue of which men possess a perfect liberty is the law of nature;
and what that law of nature does is to identify or express each man's
authority or jurisdiction over *himself, his* actions, and *his* possessions.
Although men are masterless in the state of nature in the sense that no
man is naturally subordinate to any other man, all men are subject to this
law of nature; it is essential to each man's natural freedom that all other
men are subject to this restrictive norm.

We are equals with respect to our basic rights; and since our natural
moral equality involves a lack of natural "subordination or subjection"
among us, our equality of rights must be a matter of our each equally
being non-subordinate to others. For Locke, one's non-subordination to
others does not consist merely in the absence of an obligation to submit
to others doing to one as they see fit; it includes an obligation on the
part of others not to do to one as they see fit. This natural obligation of
each individual not to subordinate others to his own will is enjoined by
the law of nature and makes our perfect freedom possible. Locke has
another way of expressing the idea that in our natural condition each
individual has a type of moral jurisdiction or authority over himself
which precludes others being at liberty to dispose of him as they see fit.

This is to say that, for each individual, there is a natural *propriety* in that individual ordering his actions and disposing of his person as he sees fit and not depending upon the leave or the will of any other. For Locke and his fellow seventeenth-century writers, to say that there is a natural propriety in one's doing as one sees fit with one's actions and person is to say that one has a natural property in one's actions and person: "... every man has a *property* in his own *person*. This no body has any right to but himself" (1980, II, 27). Rather than there being, as Hobbes maintained, no mine and thine in the state of nature, the mine-ness of oneself and the thine-ness of others is an aspect of our equal natures. The property that each person has in his own person entails that all other persons are excluded from doing as they see fit with the right-holder. This is to say that other agents are *obligated* to allow the right-holder to do as he sees fit with himself—to order his actions and dispose of his person as he chooses. Hence, the state of nature is not devoid of all obligations of men to men; it is not a moral free-for-all. Rather, our natural condition is to have rights over our own persons—over our own bodies, faculties, and actions—which all others are naturally obligated to respect.

To guard against possible misinterpretation, let us be clear that Locke is not saying that individuals in the state of nature will *in fact* always or even generally allow one another to do as they respectively see fit with their own persons and lives. He is saying that in the state of nature there is an objective moral *norm* that calls upon each individual to allow all others to dispose of themselves as they choose. Tom and John are both wandering around in an open, unclaimed, field in a region where there is no political authority. John in no way threatens Tom; yet Tom thinks it will be amusing to use his nice long stick to gouge out John's right eye, and Tom proceeds to do so. The question that primarily concerns Locke is not whether individuals in the state of nature will act in this way but, rather, whether it will be wrongful if they do so act. Locke's contention against Hobbes is that everything is *not* permissible in the absence of prohibitions issued by political authority. There are some norms which belong "to men as men" (1980, II, 14), including the norm that each has a proprietorship over himself—a norm which renders eye-gouging acts like Tom's wrongful and unjust. If one accepts the premise that our natural condition is a state of perfect freedom and Locke's argument that each person's perfect natural freedom requires that others be naturally obligated to respect that freedom, then one

should also accept his conclusion that these natural obligations exist—
as do the natural rights which are correlative to them.

The Inborn Constitution Program versus
Divine Voluntarism

Locke's most extensive discussion of the law of nature is his early and
unpublished *Essays on the Law of Nature* (*ELN*). This work lays out two
apparently conflicting views concerning the law of nature. We need to
pause to consider these views and their possible reconciliation. Locke
argues that, given God's wisdom and the fact that humans have been
created with a remarkable array of faculties, "it is quite evident that
God intends man to do *something* . . . God wills that we do *something*"
(1997, p.105, emphasis added). Yet how are we to determine what that
something is? Locke's answer is that, ". . . since man is neither made
without design nor endowed to no purpose with these faculties which
both can and must be employed, his function appears to be that which
nature has prepared him to perform" (1997, p.104, emphasis added).
We are to determine the *content* of the law of nature through an investigation of what sorts of conduct are appropriate or inappropriate to
beings with our nature, for example, with our dispositions, faculties,
vulnerabilities, and opportunities.

> . . . since man has been made such as he is, equipped with reason and
> his other faculties and destined for this mode of life, there necessarily
> result from his inborn constitution some definite duties for him, which
> cannot be other than they are. In fact, it seems to me to follow just as
> necessarily from the nature of man that, if he is a man, he is bound to
> love and worship God and also to fulfill other things appropriate to the
> rational nature, i.e., to observe the law of nature, as it follows from the
> nature of a triangle that, if it is a triangle, its three angles are equal to
> two right angles. (1997, p.125)

According to Locke, the law of nature is "the permanent rule of
morals" because it is "firmly rooted in the soil of human nature" (1997,
pp.124–5). For this reason, "human nature must needs be changed
before this law can be either altered or annulled" (1997, p.125).

. . . it follows that all those who are endowed with a rational nature, i.e., all men in the world, are morally bound by this law. In fact, this law does not depend on an unstable and changeable will, but on the eternal order of things . . . (1997, p.125)

Man's natural law duties "follow from his very nature," so that "natural law stands and falls together with the nature of man as it is at present" (1997, p.126). By the law of nature "one is bound to discharge a natural obligation, that is, to fulfill the duty which it lies upon one to perform by reason of one's nature, or else submit to the penalty due to a perpetuated crime" (1997, p.116). (The penalty will be *due* because one has failed to do *what is required by reason of one's nature.*) No amount of willing on God's part could make different moral rules apply to beings of *our* nature. It is through an inspection of man's "inborn constitution" and from inferences from that inspection that we are to identify the content of the law of nature. This is the "inborn constitution" program. When we examine Locke' arguments in the *Second Treatise* for the natural rights and correlative duties that constitute the core of the law of nature, we shall see that, in accordance with this program, he proceeds by identifying moral fertile features of our natural condition and bases his conclusions about our natural rights and duties on those features.

It is a striking thought that certain moral norms apply to us in virtue of our nature. This thought points to a question posed much earlier in the seventeenth century by the great Dutch law of nature theorist, Hugo Grotius. Would we, as the kind of beings we are, be subject to the law of nature even if God did not exist or had no concern about human affairs? Grotius gave a cautious, but revolutionary, affirmative answer to this question (2005, vol.1, p.89). Locke, I believe, *should* have given the same answer as Grotius. For, if the rule of morals is "firmly rooted in the soil of human nature," as long as that nature persists so too does that rule. However, it is also clear that were we to force Locke to answer Grotius' question, he would answer in the negative. This is because of Locke's persistent subscription to voluntarism, that is, the view that law is the command of the law maker, that the sovereign's will is the source of the law. Most saliently for Locke, God's will is the source of the law that exists independently of any earthly sovereign's will. God's commands—and not features of our nature—impose on us the law and obligations that precede the pronouncements of political authority. This is Locke's "divine voluntarism." In *ELN*, Locke tells us that

> Even if God and the soul's immorality are not moral presuppositions and laws of nature, nevertheless they must be necessarily presupposed if natural law is to exist. For there is no law without a lawmaker, and the law is to no purpose without punishment. (1997, p.113)

In a fragment "On Ethic in General" probably written in the late 1680s, Locke informs us that

> To establish morality, therefore, upon its proper basis, and such foundations as may carry an obligation with them, we must first prove a law, which always supposes a lawmaker: one that has a superiority and right to ordain and also a power to reward and punish according to the tenor of the law established by him. This sovereign lawmaker who has set rules and bounds to the actions of men is God, their maker . . . (1997, p.304)[1]

In *ECHU*, Locke asserts that "the true nature of all law" is "one intelligent being [setting] a rule to the actions of another" which is enforced by the first party's "power to reward the compliance with, and punish deviation from his rule . . ." (1959, p.475 and p.474). The relevance to Grotius' question is clear. If actions are lawful and obligatory in virtue of God's willing us to perform them or, perhaps, God's threatening to punish our failure to perform them, then were God to go out of existence or to cease to be concerned with human affairs, all lawfulness—indeed, it seems, all morality—would go out of existence.

To be fair, Locke does continually seek a more subtle version of divine voluntarism than the stark claim that whatever God *arbitrarily* wills is, for that reason, lawful and obligatory. In the *ELN*, Locke tells us that part of the explanation for why we are obligated by God's will is that God possesses "divine wisdom." So, ". . . it is reasonable that we should do what shall please him who is omniscient and most wise" (1997, p.117). In the passage from "On Ethic in General," Locke insists that God can function as lawmaker only because he has both superiority and *right*. Moreover, Locke repeatedly advances a further basis for the authority of God's decrees, viz., that God is our creator and "all things are justly subject to that by which they have first been made" (1997, p.117). So, contrary to the spirit of voluntarism, God's authority itself depends upon the principle that creators have authority over what they have created—a principle that could not itself flow from his authority. Finally, in *ECHU*, Locke explains that God has a right to promulgate norms for us because

. . . we are his creatures: he has goodness and wisdom to direct our actions to that which is best: and he has power to enforce by rewards and punishments of infinite weight and duration in another life. (1959, II, p.475)

Even though Locke mentions God's power to reward and punish, the importance of this power here is that it insures that God's promulgation of norms will not be in vain (1959, II, p.474).

Moreover, we can see how divine voluntarism—whether it focuses on God's raw will and power or his wise exercise of authority—can be wielded against Filmer's and Hobbes' *legal* voluntarism. God's will simply trumps the earthly sovereign's will. It is God's will which establishes what is lawful and unlawful; so, the basic measure of whether an individual acts lawfully or unlawfully is whether he abides by or deviates from God's will. This measure applies to the actions and the decrees of earthly sovereigns. Hence, actions or decrees by an earthly sovereign that contravene God's decrees are actually unlawful. A subject who refuses to abide by or even resists an unlawful command of his earthly sovereign may indeed be acting lawfully, that is, in accord with the *real* sovereign's will.[2] All that needs to be added to divine voluntarism to get to the conclusion that subjects may sometimes refuse to abide by enacted law or even resist its enforcement and dispose of its earthly source is the belief—which is rejected by Filmer and Hobbes—that it makes sense for individuals to judge for themselves in these matters.

Whatever the subtleties of divine voluntarism and its uses against errant and willful earthly sovereigns, *if* divine voluntarism is a second program for identifying the contents of the law of nature, then Locke is in philosophical trouble. For then we would have one program which says that the key to the law of nature lies in identifying crucial features of human existence on the basis of which we each have reasons to follow certain norms in our interactions with others and another program which says that the key to the law of nature lies in identifying God's commands to us concerning our interactions with others. In the one case, how we have reason to act turns on our inborn human constitution; in the other case, it is God's will which determines how we should conduct ourselves. In the first case, when we appeal to the law of nature to condemn a willful earthly ruler, we are appealing to norms "derived from nature" (1997, p.88). In the second case, we appeal to God's higher, more authoritative will; the norms do not derive from nature; rather they are artifacts imposed upon us by God's (perhaps wise and all-knowing) commands. It is precisely because there is, on the voluntarist view, no *natural* moral order that the sovereign—be it God or some earthly sovereign or both—has to get busy issuing decrees which *inject* an artificial moral order into the world.³ In the *Second Treatise*, in accordance with the inborn constitution program, Locke insists that the law of nature is essentially a matter of reason (1980, II, 5, 8, 10, & 30). It is reason which detects and articulates the norms which we have reason to abide by and it is our rational nature on which these norms rests. If, in contrast, norms are valid for us because God wills us to follow them, then the law of nature is essentially a matter of will, not of reason.

Moreover, *if* the divine voluntarist doctrine is a second program for identifying the contents of the law of nature, it is a program that Locke cannot and does not attempt to carry out. It is a program that he cannot carry out because, according to Locke, we cannot have the access to God's mind and intentions that it requires. According to Locke, the law of nature is known "by the light of nature"; and this means that a man can attain knowledge of it 'by himself and without the help of another, if he makes proper use of the faculties he is endowed with by nature." Those faculties are "understanding, reason, and self-perception" (1997, p.89). In *ELN* and much more elaborately in *ECHU*, Locke holds that all knowledge begins with sense perception and then develops through "reason and the power of arguing" (1997, p.94). We cannot by the light of nature have anything like direct access to God's mind and intentions. Locke's general epistemological stance rules out identifying the content of the law of nature by appeal to revelation or by some sort of direct inspection of God's mind and intentions.

All of this suggests that Locke's divine voluntarism is *not* a second program for identifying the contents of the law of nature. So what role does it play within Locke's understanding of the law of nature? Here is a very natural and *almost* satisfactory answer. The inborn constitution program does the heavy lifting of identifying the norms that we have reason to comply with. The divine voluntarist doctrine then comes along to explain why those norms are obligatory laws. They are obligatory laws because God wills that we act in accordance with the norms that we have reason to abide by. God's will *adds* the qualities of lawfulness and obligatoriness to the norms which are to be identified through the inborn constitution program. This would be a very nice reconciliation of the inborn constitution program and the divine voluntarist doctrine except for two difficulties.

The first difficulty is that it is far from clear that Locke himself distinguishes the task of identifying the dictates of reason from the task of explaining why those dictates are obligatory laws of conduct. He never answers Grotius' question by saying that, if God did not exist, there would still be dictates of reason for us to abide by—albeit they would not be obligatory laws. When Locke considers whether atheists should be tolerated, he does not say that atheists will not recognize the obligatory lawfulness of keeping promises but may well recognize that promise-keeping is a dictate of reason. When Locke enters into his divine voluntarist line of thought, he seems to cast off the idea that an investigation of our inborn constitution can provide us with reasoned guidance for how we should behave. He seems to expect all guidance to come from some sort of direct detection of how God wills us to act.[4]

The second difficulty is a philosophical problem within the proposed reconciliation. Presumably God commands in accordance with the dictates of reason. That is, he commands humans to abide by a given norm if and only if men have reasons which "follow from [their] nature" (1997, p.126) to abide by that norm. Our question then is, How does God's command *add* obligatoriness to the norm? One possibility is that it is the prospect of divine punishment for violating the norm which makes the norm obligatory (and, hence, makes the norm a law). But, at least in *ELN*, Locke quite reasonably rejects this connection between God's willing that we follow that norm and our being obligated to follow it. The threat of punishment for noncompliance in itself cannot produce a genuine obligation to follow the norm. Such a threat can coerce one to follow the norm, just as a pirate or robber can through various threats coerce one to do as he pleases (1997, p.116). But coercion does not produce a genuine *obligation* to act in the way one is compelled to act. For genuine obligation to exist, *conscience* must be bound and coercion (via threats of punishment) cannot bind conscience. The only thing which can bind conscience with respect to a given norm and, thereby, produce an obligation to abide by that norm is a grasp of the *reasons* for complying with that norm. As Locke puts it, ". . . all obligation binds conscience and lays a bound on the mind itself, so that not fear of punishment, but a rational apprehension of what is right, puts us under an obligation . . ." (1997, p.118). In *ELN*, Locke sharply distinguishes between acting on the basis of reason and acting out of fear of punishment (1997, p.117). The latter, of course, can also be reasonable; but it is not a matter of acting on the basis of a rational apprehension of the rightness of the action in question. Hence, it is not a matter of obligatory conduct.

If the prospect of punishment for violating a norm does not add obligatoriness to it, it seems that it must be God's *endorsement* of the norm that does the trick. God, presumably, sees that this norm is a dictate of reason for humans; and, on that basis, he endorses humans abiding by this norm. The difficulty is that it is hard to see how any individual's belief that God endorses this norm can add to his rational appreciation of the norm and, thereby, add to his being bound in conscience to abide by the norm. If God endorses the norm because individuals have reason to abide by it, then saying that God endorses the norm adds nothing to individuals' rational appreciation for the norm. Thus, if we are obligated to abide by norms that God endorses, that obligation must derive from our rational appreciation for those norms and not from something which is added by God's endorsement of them. God's endorsement of the norm is an unnecessary extra wheel in the explanation for why we are bound in conscience and are genuinely obligated to abide by norms for which we have a rational appreciation. The explanation for our being bound in conscience and obligated to abide by a norm is simply that we see the norm as a dictate of reason. Locke's own understanding of what it means to be obligated, viz., that it is to be bound in conscience by one's rational appreciation, should lead Locke to see that, once we recognize a norm as a dictate of reason, we should conclude that we have a *natural* obligation to abide by it. Locke himself comes very close to saying this when he writes that

. . . by the bond of law we must mean here the bound of natural law whereby one is bound to discharge a natural obligation, that is, to fulfill a duty which lies upon one's person *by reason of one's nature*, or else submit to the penalty due to a perpetrated crime. (1997, p.116)[5]

My conclusion is that Locke has no *good* reason to appeal to his divine voluntarism within his theory of the law of nature. He does have a reason, viz., his general commitment to the idea that law must proceed from the will of a law giver. Yet this doctrine that authority is the source of law and, hence, cannot itself be subject to law is more suited to authoritarian than liberal political theory. Indeed, Locke's own early and authoritarian *Second Tract on Government* (1997) is an extraordinary expression of the view that right and wrong have to be injected—by successive acts of will—into a world which is otherwise devoid of all right and wrong. Locke's voluntarism seems to be the one important element of his early authoritarian stance that Locke retains throughout his life. So, clearly, I am not denying the ongoing presence of divine voluntarism in Locke's writings and thought. I am contending that the best construal of his arguments for natural rights will present those arguments as developments of an inborn constitution program that does not need to be supplemented by divine voluntarism. The benefit of this conclusion is that it frees Locke's key arguments within political theory from dependence upon the theological premises associated with divine voluntarism. Hence, a positive assessment of those arguments does not depend upon the acceptance of those premises.

The Rational Pursuit of Happiness, Moral Equality, and the Reciprocity Argument

So we turn now to the crucial features of the human condition on which, according to the inborn constitution program, the basic norms of the law of nature rest. The twofold first feature is that each person pursues his own happiness *and* that it accords with reason for each to pursue his own happiness. Although, this is a view that Locke did not hold in his early *ELN*, he subscribed to it with striking consistency from the mid-1670s onward. Indeed, from that time onward, Locke expressed this doctrine in highly hedonistic language. Ultimately individuals seek pleasure and avoid pain; and that is what they have reason to seek and to avoid. In a fragment now labeled, 'Pleasure, Pain, the Passions,' Locke tells us that pleasure and pain "are the two roots out of which all passions spring and a centre on which they all turn" (1997, p.237).[6] "To love, then, is nothing but to have in our mind the idea of something which we consider as capable to produce satisfaction or delight in us" (1997, p.238). Often when we seem to love a friend, we really just take pleasure in what the friend can provide to us. But, sometimes, we do directly take pleasure in another's well-being. For instance, nature ". . . has made us so that we are delighted with the very being of our children" (1997, p.239).[7] What explains our pursuit of the well-being of our children and makes that pursuit reasonable is its contribution to our own happiness. Whether our focus is on eternal happiness or the "very imperfect' idea of happiness in this world, it is 'inexcusable' and 'of the greatest folly, if we use not our greatest care and endeavors to obtain it" (1997, p.242).

In an extraordinary fragment from the late 1670s now labeled 'Morality,' Locke asserts that,

> Morality is the rule of man's actions for the attaining happiness.
> For the end and aim of all men being happiness alone, nothing could be a rule or a law to them whose observation did not lead to happiness and whose breach did [not] draw misery after it. (1997, p.267)

Although "it is possible there may be a state after this life wherein men may be capable of enjoyments or suffering," we can ask especially "[a]s to this life . . . what is the way of attainment of pleasure and avoiding of pain . . ." (1997, p.268). In another fragment ("Thus, I Think") composed shortly before the publication of the *Two Treatises*, we again find Locke endorsing each individual's pursuit of his long-term happiness.

> 'Tis a man's proper business to seek happiness and avoid misery. Happiness consists in what delights and contents the mind, misery in what disturbs, discomposes or torments it. I will therefore make it my business to seek satisfaction and delight and avoid uneasiness and disquiet and to have as much of the one and as little of the other as may be. But here I must have a care I mistake not, for if I prefer a short pleasure to a lasting one, 'tis plain I cross my own happiness. (1997, p.296)

Finally, in *ECHU*, Locke tells us that all good, that is, all happiness, is "the proper object of desire in general." Nevertheless, not every instance of happiness in general moves each particular man's desire; each man is moved only by those instances of happiness "which make a necessary part of *his* happiness."

> All other good, however great in reality or appearance, excites not a man's desires who looks not on it to make a part of that happiness

wherewith he, in his present thoughts, can satisfy himself. Happiness, under this view, everyone constantly pursues, and desires what make any part of it: other things, acknowledged to be good, he can look upon without desire, pass by, and be content without (1959, II, p.341).

For Locke, however, each man's pursuit of happiness is not a matter of each man's being driven by the force of present desires. For the mind has the great capacity "to *suspend* the execution and satisfaction of any of its desires."

> . . . a man may *suspend* the act of his choice from being determined for or against the thing proposed, till he has examined whether it be really of a nature, in itself and consequences, to make him happy or not. (1959, II, pp.352–3)

We may reflect upon our individual desires and their objects and come to a critical judgment about what desires we will individually endorse and pursue. When we have done this, "we have done our duty, all that we can, or ought to do, in pursuit of our happiness . . ." (1959, II, p.345). Our natural orientation toward our own happiness is, according to Locke, no abridgement of our metaphysical liberty. For this liberty consists in our being able to reflect upon alternative courses of action toward happiness and to judge which course shall be taken. For each individual, this liberty consists in the fact that "by his constitution as an intelligent being" he is "determined in willing by his own thought and judgment what is best for him to do: else he would be under the determination of some other than himself, which is want of liberty" (1959, II, p.346).

We have already encountered the second crucial feature of our inborn constitution in our discussion of Locke's understanding of our perfect natural freedom. That feature is our natural moral equality. One aspect or implication of this natural moral equality is that, whatever moral claims or rights one individual has against other agents, each other agent has against that first individual. In our state of natural equality "all power [i.e., right] and jurisdiction is reciprocal" (1980, II, 4). For each individual, the equal standing of others as beings who reasonably look to their own happiness constrains how that individual ought to advance his own good. An extremely interesting statement of this contention appears in Locke's fragment on "Morality."

All men being equally under one and the same rule, if it be permitted to me to break my word for my advantage it is also permitted everyone else, and then whatever I possess will be subject to the force or deceit of all the rest of the men in the world, in which state it is impossible for any man to be happy unless he were both stronger and wiser than all the rest of mankind, for in such a state of rapine and force it is impossible any one man should be master of those things whose possession is necessary to his well being. (1997, pp.268–9)

We can distinguish between a pragmatic and a conceptual reading of this passage. On the pragmatic reading, one is concerned with the factual consequences of engaging in deceit or the use of force against others. Here the troublesome consequence of my engaging in such conduct towards others is their *actually treating me* in a similar fashion. Unless one is "stronger and wiser" than all the rest of mankind, this response on the part of others will leave me worse off than I would be had I not triggered their deceit or force by my own deceit or force. Since one is not stronger and wiser than the rest of mankind, engaging in deceit or force is an imprudent policy. However, it is clear that Locke is seeking more than the conclusion that prudence counsels one to avoid using force or deception on others. He is seeking the conclusion that each of us is committed to others' having *rights* against being subjected to deceit or force. This conclusion is provided by the conceptual construal of this passage. On this construal, one is concerned with the logical implications of one's being permitted to break one's word to others or to subject others to force. Since all men are equally under one and the same rule, if one is permitted to act in these ways toward others, others are equally permitted to use force or deceit against one. So, if one wants to hold that others are not permitted to use force or deceit against one, one must as a matter of consistency deny that one is permitted to use force or deceit against others. The logical cost of affirming one's own right not to be subjected to force or deceit is one's acknowledgement of others' equal right.

The reciprocity argument reappears in the *Second Treatise* when Locke begins to explain why there is a law of nature. Locke presents a passage from Richard Hooker's *Ecclesiastical Polity* which is not so much about love as about the logic of reciprocity.

. . . if I do harm, I must look to suffer, there being no reason that others should shew greater measure of love to me, than they have by me,

shewed unto them; my desire therefore to be lov'd of my equals in
nature, as much as possible may be, imposeth upon me a natural duty
of bearing to them-ward, fully the like affection; from which relation of
equality between our selves and them, that are as our selves, what
several rules and canons, natural reason hath drawn for direction of
life, no man is ignorant. (1980, II, 5)

This passage from Hooker can also be read as a pragmatic or as
a conceptual argument. As a pragmatic argument, it declares that unloving behavior toward others will in fact call forth unloving behavior
from others. If one wants to induce loving behavior from others, one had
better act lovingly toward them. As a conceptual argument, it declares
that, if one is to make a reasonable claim upon others' loving treatment
of one, one must recognize the reasonableness of their like claims against
oneself.

If we substitute into the Hooker passage two premises that Locke
clearly has in mind, the conceptual version of the Hooker passage
becomes an argument for each person's rational commitment to others'
possessing against them rights to freedom. One premise is that the
condition which each individual desires with respect to every other
individual is not love, but freedom—understood as the right to dispose
of one's actions and person as one sees fit. The second premise is that,
for each individual, this is a rational desire. Each of us rationally desires
freedom vis-a-vis all other persons because, in our interactions with
others, freedom is the crucial condition for self-preservation. "He that,
in the state of nature, *would take away the freedom* that belongs to any one
in that state, must necessarily be supposed to have a design to take away
every thing else, that freedom being the foundation of all the rest" (1980,
II, 17). Furthermore, we rationally desire self-preservation because it is
the essential precondition of happiness. If we substitute the rational
interest in freedom for Hooker's interest in love and formulate the reciprocity argument conceptually, we get something like:

Each man rationally lays claim to freedom in his relationships with
all other men. Each rationally asserts for himself a right to freedom.
However, we are equals in nature and therefore are equally under the
same rule. Thus, each man has to acknowledge that, if he has a right to
freedom, so too do all other men have this right. The logical cost of
affirming one's own right to freedom is the acknowledgement of
others' rights to freedom. Since, even given this cost of asserting a

right to freedom on his own behalf, each man does have reason to assert that right, each man is committed in reason to affirming the rights of all men against having their freedom infringed.

Putting aside the freedom of disposing of one's *possessions* as one sees fit until we get to Locke's discussion of property, this right against having one's freedom infringed is the core natural law right of self-proprietorship. The correlative to that right is the core natural law duty not to trespass upon others' self-proprietorship.

The Workmanship of God, the False Presumption, and the Like Reason Arguments

In the section of chapter II that follows the passage from Hooker, Locke offers three further arguments for the same natural right to freedom or, alternatively put, to self-ownership. Two of those arguments—one of which I have put in bold—are contained in the passage that follows Locke's assertion that the state of nature has a law of nature to govern it.

> . . . being all *equal and independent*, no one ought to harm another in his life, health, liberty, or possessions: **for men being all the workmanship of one omnipotent, and infinitely wise maker; all the servants of one sovereign master, sent into the world by his order and about his business, they are his property, whose workmanship they are, made to last during his, not one another's pleasure**. And being furnished with like faculties, sharing all in one community of nature, there cannot be supposed any such *subordination* among us, that may authorize us to destroy one another, as if we were made for one another's uses, as the inferior ranks of creatures are for our's. (1980, II, 6)

The center portion of this passage provides us with the "workmanship" argument—an argument that brings God, but *not* voluntarism, back into the picture. We have already encountered the premise that the creator of any object has rights over that object in our discussion of divine voluntarism. We shall see this premise again within Locke's discussion of why human beings have rights over the objects *they* have created. In the present case, the premise about the rights of creators over their creations plus the premise that God created us yield the conclusion that we are each the property of God. It is because we are each the property of God that no individual may destroy another individual; for that would be a trespass upon *God's* property. Indeed, any individual's *self*-destruction will also be an infringement upon God's rights over that individual. Let us see why this "workmanship" argument works very poorly as an argument about human rights and yet serves other important purposes for Locke.

The main problem with the workmanship argument is that it does not at all advance the conclusion that *individuals* have rights against other individuals not to be destroyed or maimed or enslaved by them. For, on the basis of this argument, the only agent whose rights are infringed when Tom destroys John is *God*. In contrast, the conclusion which Locke wants to reach is that each individual is a *self-owner*; hence, whenever an individual is destroyed (except as a matter of just defense or punishment), *that individual* is wronged by the destroyer. Moreover, the conclusion that we are all the property of God conflicts with numerous other claims that Locke wishes to advance. Locke wants to say that while Tom is engaged in his effort to kill poor John, John is entirely at liberty to kill Tom and others are morally free to come to his assistance. Furthermore, should Tom succeed in killing John, any other individual in the state of nature would be morally free to punish Tom even to the point of destroying him. Yet why think that God's ownership of Tom diminishes in the course of his attack on John or in the aftermath of his success? Why think that Tom's attacking or killing John is a way of Tom's liberating himself from ownership by God? If, however, Tom remains the property of God, then John's act of self-defensive killing would be a violation of God's right over Tom—as would be the retributive killing of Tom by John's avenger. Locke's appeal to the theological principle that each person is the workmanship of God not only leaves each person without rights *of his own* against being killed, maimed, or enslaved by others, it also undermines Locke's claim that persons possess rights to engage in defense and punishment.

Why then does Locke offer the workmanship argument? Locke wants to say that, absent very special circumstances, individuals do not have a right to commit suicide; and the doctrine of God's ownership of us provides a rationale for saying this. Locke also has an important use for the workmanship argument within his political theory. The argument is used to undercut the view—found, for example, in Hobbes' account of sovereignty by institution—that unlimited political authority has been created by individuals transferring all of their natural rights to some earthly sovereign. Locke holds that no such total divestment of rights has in fact occurred; he thinks that men are too rational to engage in such a divestiture. However, Locke wants to make the stronger claim that no such total transfer of rights is *possible*. He does this by arguing that no one can convey any right to an aspiring sovereign which that agent does not originally possess over himself. Since we are God's property, we do not possess rights to destroy, maim, or enslave ourselves and, hence, we *cannot* convey any such right to aspiring sovereign ". . . [H]e that cannot take away his own life, cannot give another power over it . . ." (1980, II, 23). Thus, the sort of transfer of rights envisioned by authoritarian contract theorists such as Hobbes is impossible.[8] The only problem for Locke is that, if we are really God's property and all our seeming rights are really God's rights, then we cannot transfer *any* of the rights which *seem* to be ours in the state of nature. Hence, *no* rise of political authority by way of contract is possible! My conclusion, therefore, is that Locke's workmanship argument, like his divine voluntarism, is unhelpful to his main line of reasoning. We should not seek to integrate either the workmanship argument or his divine voluntarism into the basic structure of his political doctrine.[9]

If we look at the sentences that surround the workmanship argument in the passage above, we will detect another argument—the false presumption argument—that can readily be integrated into Locke's central doctrine. Once again Locke appeals to our natural equality; there is a community of nature among us.[10] However, a further premise appears, viz., that actions by any agent which subordinate another individual to that agent's will presume that the subordinated individual exists to serve the purposes of the subordinating agent. However, given our natural moral equality, no individual exists for the purposes of any other individual. Since the presumption implicated in all such acts of subordination is false, all such actions are unjustified, contrary to right. Do we have any reason beyond our natural equality to say that no individual exists for the purposes of any other? Part of the appeal to Locke of the workmanship argument is that it supplies us with such a reason; no man exists for any other man's purposes because all men exist for God's purposes. Yet, as we have seen, this takes us down some troublesome paths. There is, however, *another* basis for holding that each individual exists for his own purposes. This is Locke's doctrine that each individual has in his own happiness an ultimate purpose for his own actions.

Immediately following the last passage presented from Locke, we are presented with a fifth argument for a natural right against deprivations of freedom. I have called this the like reason argument. As Locke states it,

Every one, as he is *bound to preserve himself,* and not quite his station wilfully, so by the like reason, when his preservation comes not in competition, ought he, as much as he can, *to preserve the rest of mankind,* and may not unless it be to do justice on an offender, take away, or impair the life, or what tends to the preservation of the life, the liberty, health, limb, or goods of another. (1980, II, 6)

To understand this argument we need to begin by not misunderstanding its conclusion. Locke initially states his conclusion in terms of the preservation of the rest of mankind. Some commentators have taken this language—which Locke repeats throughout the *Second Treatise*—to show that Locke took the fundamental law of nature to mandate the maximum aggregate preservation of human lives.[11] Yet this understanding will not stand; and it is important to see why it won't stand.

First, when Locke speaks of the preservation of the rest of mankind he often immediately adds a more detailed statement of what he means by this preservation; and that more detailed statement is that no one is to infringe upon others' freedoms, no one is to invade another or do another harm. Such an explicating statement appears in the passage above: unless it is to do justice to an offender, no one is to "take away, or impair the life, or what tends to the preservation of the life, the liberty, health, limb, or goods of another." In the very next sentence Locke says that the law of nature "which willeth the peace and *preservation of all mankind*" is observed when all men are "restrained from invading others rights, and from doing hurt to one another" (1980, II, 7). In the *First Treatise,* Locke tells us that government "for the good of the governed" is government "for the Preservation of every Mans Right and Property, by preserving him from the Violence or Injury of others."[12] Way back in Locke's earliest liberal essay, "An Essay on Toleration," Locke tells us that the magistrate's authority to act for "the good of the public . . . only protects [men] from being invaded and injured in them by others (which is a perfect toleration)" (1997, pp.137–8).

Second, only if the conclusion of the like reason argument is that each has a right against his life, liberty, health, limb or goods being taken away or impaired does this argument line up with the other arguments we have canvassed—which conclude that individuals are not to suffer subordination, are not to have their freedom infringed, are not to have their rights invaded.

Third, the view that the fundamental law of nature calls for the maximal aggregate preservation of mankind conflicts with Locke's consistent view that the pursuit by individuals of *their own* happiness and self-preservation is a deeply embedded feature of *rational* human action. We have already documented Locke's endorsement of each individual's pursuit of his own happiness. The counterpart to that in Locke's political writings is Locke's recognition and acceptance of self-preservation as the primary human motivation. In the *First Treatise*, Locke tells us that self-preservation is "[t]he first and strongest desire God Planted in Men, and wrought into the very Principles of their Nature . . ." (1960, I, 88). In the *Second Treatise*, he tells us that men rationally enter into society to rid themselves of those "who invade [the] fundamental, sacred, and unalterable law of *self-preservation*" (1980, II, 149).

Fourth, Locke's investigation of the fundamental law of nature is simply not a search for some common end, for example, the preservation of all mankind, which will serve as the ultimate guide for human action. *Locke's investigation is of an entirely different nature.* It is an inquiry about natural *authority*. Is there natural authority and, if there is, who has it over what? It is because it is an inquiry first and foremost about natural authority that Locke begins with the state of nature; and this is also why his fundamental conclusion is that in the state of nature, each man is "absolute lord of his own person and possessions, equal to the greatest, and subject to no body" (1980, II, 123).

So what is going on within the like reason argument? I believe that Locke is asking the question, What is each individual to make of the fact that, just as he ought or is even obligated to preserve himself, by like reason every other individual ought or is even obligated to preserve himself? What is one to make of the fact that all these other persons are also centers of value; they also have in their own happiness and self-preservation ends which they would be greatly foolish not to seek? (1959, I, p.242) There seem to be three possible answers to this question.

One answer is that one is to make nothing of this fact; this is the "no import" (and Hobbesian) response. The fact that John ought or is even obligated to preserve himself in itself has no practical import for Tom. Even though John has proper and reasonable ends of his own and does not, like lower creatures and material resources, exist for the purposes of other persons, for example, Tom, this fact about John has no bearing on how it is reasonable for Tom to behave toward John. Just as Tom may use lower creatures and material resources in whatever ways best suit his purposes, so too may Tom use John in whatever ways best suit Tom's purposes. Another answer—at the other end of the spectrum of answers—is that Tom should treat the ends which John has reason to promote as ends which he too has (equal) reason to promote. The thought is that, since John's ends (his happiness and self-preservation) are rational ends, reason requires that Tom add those ends to the list of ends which he has reason to promote; this is the "adoption response." Because John has reason to promote certain ends, Tom ought also to adopt those ends.

The no import response seems to be too little. For surely the fact that there are these other beings who are as much centers of value as one-self—who as much have purposes of their own that they have reason to devote themselves to achieve—has got to have *some sort* of impact on how one conducts oneself toward these beings. These facts about these other beings have got to provide us with reason to be *in some way* more circumspect in our treatment of them than we are in our treatment of lower creatures and material resources. However, the adoption response seems to be too much. The import for Tom of the fact that John has reason to promote John's happiness and self-preservation is not that Tom has reason to promote John's happiness and self-preservation. Recall here Locke's claim from the *ECHU* that, although everyone's happiness is in a sense part of the good of happiness, each individual desires and is rational in pursuing "only that part, or so much of it as is considered and taken to make a necessary part of his happiness" (1959, I, p.341). What third answer is available which will neither make too little nor too much of the fact that other humans by like reason ought to seek their happiness and self-preservation?

That third answer seems to be that, although one does not adopt other persons' ends as ends one is to promote, one does avoid pursuing one's own ends in ways that prevent others from devoting themselves to the pursuit of their respective ends. Others' existence as separate centers of value, as beings who, like oneself, ought to promote their respective happiness and self-preservation does call for some form of circumspection in one's conduct toward them. And the apt form of that circumspection is avoidance of action that deprives any of these other beings of their freedom to dispose of their own actions and persons as they see fit in the service of their ends. The practical import for Tom of all those other individuals being by the like reason obligated to pursue their own happiness or self-preservation is a natural obligation on Tom's part not to deprive them of their freedom to dispose of their actions and persons as they see fit. Correlative to that duty is a natural right of each of these individuals against Tom that he not deprive them of freedom. That right, which Tom also possesses, is the "property [every man has] in his own *person*" (1980, II, 27). It is the structure of natural authority in which, although no man is master of any other man, each man is "master of himself and *proprietor of his own person* . . . ." (1980, II, 44).

The intersection of the perfect freedom, reciprocity, false presumption, and like reason arguments constitutes a powerful case for a natural right to freedom which, given Locke's understanding of freedom, is also a natural right of self-proprietorship. The essential intuition which is articulated through these arguments is that, in virtue of our inborn constitution, human beings are moral equals who come into the world as neither masters or servants to one another, who rationally lay claim to rights to freedom against one another and are rationally committed to affirming like rights in their moral equals, who each rationally seek their own happiness and self-preservation and take appropriate cognizance of each others' rational devotion of his own person to his own happiness and self-preservation by recognizing that, while he has natural moral authority over himself, each other person has a like authority over himself. Insofar as one thinks that this inborn constitution is God's wise design, one can *add* that, through the creation of us with the nature we have, God has ordained that we achieve the good of happiness and has especially arranged things so that each individual is rationally charged with the achievement of his own happiness and with allowing each other individual to pursue his own happiness.

According to Locke, not only are there good arguments for an original right of self-proprietorship, but individuals in the state of nature do at least to some degree recognize these rights in themselves and in others. Moreover, this rational appreciation of one another's rights has some motivational force for people. All—or at least most—persons in the state of nature have some disposition to respect the rights of others and take most other persons also to have that disposition. This mutual disposition to respect rights, combined with a certain level of natural sociability, checks the suspicion and rush to preemptive attack which otherwise turn the state of nature into a war of all against all. According to Locke, individuals in the state of nature are sufficiently moved to abide by the natural moral order that obtains among men as men that they need not throw themselves upon the mercy of a Hobbesian sovereign.

Reason, Motivation, and Compliance with the Law of Nature

The inborn constitution program reveals reasons we have not to infringe upon the freedom of others to dispose of their persons and actions as they see fit. These dictates of reason, rather than calculations of reward or punishment, *obligate us* (*bind us in conscience*) to eschew the unprovoked killing, enslaving, or maiming of others. It may be that one's respect for others' rights—at least if it is reciprocated by others— *also* serves one's happiness. Indeed, Locke maintains that participation in a system of reciprocal respect for individual freedom is, for each member of society, his best bet for achieving happiness.

> . . . every one should not only allow, but recommend and magnify those rules to others, from whose observance of them he is sure to reap advantage to himself. He may, out of *interest* as well as *conviction*, cry up that for sacred, which, if once trampled on and profaned, he himself cannot be safe nor secure. (1959, I, p.70, emphasis added)

Nevertheless, the happiness payoff which one may get from respect for others' rights is distinct from the rational appreciation of others' equal moral standing which grounds one's *obligation* not to infringe upon others' freedom and their *rights* against that infringement. It looks like Locke should say that there are two distinct kinds of reasons for being circumspect in one's treatment of others. There are obligating (conscience-binding) reasons which derive from our inborn nature as equal and independent beings; to abide by these reasons is to act out of *conviction*. And there are payoff reasons which derive from the happiness one is likely to get from not infringing on others' freedom; to abide by these reasons is to act out of *interest*. Indeed, Locke essentially makes this distinction in *ELN* when he contrasts persons abiding by the law of nature because they have "a rational apprehension of what is right, [which] puts them under an obligation . . ." (1997, p.118) and abiding by the law of nature to avoid punishments or, presumably, to attain rewards (1997, p.117).

Yet at least from the mid-1670s Locke seems to hold that the only thing which can provide any of us with rational motivation to act in a given way is the prospect of a happiness payoff. Recall, for example, his claim from in *ECHU*.

> All other good, however great in reality or appearance, excites not a man's desires who looks not on it to make a part of that happiness wherewith he, in his present thoughts, can satisfy himself. Happiness, under this view, everyone constantly pursues, and desires what make any part of it: other things, acknowledged to be good, he can look upon without desire, pass by, and be content without. (1959, II, p.341)

This makes all reasons matters of the agent's interest in his happiness. However, this reduction of *all* reasons to considerations of the agent's happiness is problematic for Locke. For it will follow that the only reason any agent has to respect others' rights is the happiness which this will (we presume) yield for that agent. This runs counter to the central Lockean thought that is embedded in all of the *Second Treatise*'s arguments for natural rights (except the workmanship argument), viz., that to recognize others' rights is to recognize reasons to be constrained in one's conduct toward them which *flow from other persons being equal and independent agents*. The rights others have against one are the directive import of their being agents like oneself who have ultimate purposes of their own. It is because the reasons one has for constraint are grounded in facts about the right-holders—not in facts about the conduciveness of the constraint to one's happiness—that one's constraint is *owed* to the right-holders.[13]

Still, if reciprocal respect for rights is each individual's best bet for achieving happiness, would not each individual's sensible and single-minded pursuit of his own happiness yield reciprocal respect for rights and, hence, every individuals' happiness? If everyone's happiness is promoted by general compliance with the laws of nature, why bother finding some further, obligatory basis for compliance? Locke poses this question to himself in the last essay of *ELN*, "Is Every Man's Own Interest the Basis of the Law of Nature?" For, although Locke there denies that the law of nature is *based upon* self-interest, he quickly adds that general compliance with right action is highly conducive to individual advantage.

> . . . when we say that each man's person interest is not the basis of natural law, we do not wish to be understood to say that the common rules of human equity and each man's private interest are opposed to one another, for . . . without the observance of [the law of nature] it is impossible for anybody to be master of his property and to pursue his own advantage. . . . [N]othing contributes so much to the general welfare of each and so effectively keeps men's possessions safe and secure as the observance of natural law. (1997, pp.128–9)

So, again, why not think that the simple motive of promoting happiness will at least get us to mutually beneficial general compliance? Here, I think, is Locke's answer: If we each perceive ourselves and others as rationally motivated only by anticipations of our own advantage, we each will comply with the laws of nature only if we have good reason to expect others will reciprocally comply. But, if we each perceive others and are perceived by others as likely to comply only if they or ourselves have good reason to expect others to comply, we will each rationally suspect that some other agents will not comply. And the fact that we will each know that we each rationally suspect that some other agents will not comply itself will heighten our rational expectation that some of us will not comply and, thereby, will undermine in each of our cases the rationality of our compliance with the laws of nature. This, of course, is the sort of spiral of suspicion that operates among men in a Hobbesian state of nature, that is, among rational men who are moved only by considerations of their own advantage, who would all benefit from mutual compliance with norms which Hobbes calls "laws of nature," but who cannot get to that compliance because they have no assurance of one another's compliance.

What Locke needs and has to check that spiral and to act as a catalyst for reciprocal respect for one another's rights is the idea that we do each have reasons to recognize others' rights and that this "rational apprehension of what is right" (1997, p.118) itself has some motivational force for us. If and only if men think of themselves as having reasons, obligations, and rights which are revealed by the inborn constitution arguments will they reciprocally comply with those rights and each get the desired happiness payoff. This, I think, is the deep insight which appears near the close of *ELN* when Locke responds to the "objector" who says that, if general compliance does serve everyone's utility, "then the basis of natural law is each man's own interest." Locke's response is that

> . . . utility is not the basis of the law or the ground of obligation, but the consequence of obedience to it . . . And thus the rightness of an action does not depend on its utility, on the contrary, its utility is a result of its rightness. (1997, p.133)

This, of course, is not to say that all men *will* voluntarily respect all other men's rights. For not all men are rational. Those men will have to be given the sort of reason for compliance which threats of punishment provide.

More State of Nature Rights

State of nature rights are moral rights that we possess or can acquire independent of any social compact and any exercise of governmental authority. According to Locke, these rights extend beyond our natural right to dispose of our own person and actions as we see fit. Among our other natural rights is each individual's right that others abide by the promises and bargains they have made with him. Correlative to this natural right is the natural obligation to keep one's promises and compacts. Particular agreements among men within the state of nature—*including any agreements to exit the state of nature*—are binding because and only because ". . . truth and keeping of faith belongs to men as men . . ." (1980, II, 14). Locke provides a considerably more extensive discussion of our natural rights to act as executors of the law of nature. And he proceeds on to an even more extensive and influential account of the acquisition of private property rights within the state of nature. In connection with this account of property rights, Locke delineates certain limitations ("provisos"[1]) on property rights and how extensively these provisos are satisfied as money comes into use and as commerce develops. In the first section of this chapter, I briefly discussion that natural right to enforce the law of nature. Sections two and three articulate Locke's basic account of private property rights. Sections four and five deal with the introduction of money, the expansion of commerce, and the ways in which the provisos are circumvented or satisfied. Section six relates Locke's endorsement of the "enough and as good" proviso to his late (1697) essay on the poor law (1997, pp.182–98).

The Right to Act as Executor of the Law of Nature

Locke holds that the law of nature would in practice come to nothing if there were no right to enforce it in the state of nature. Since all men are equal in the state of nature, if anyone has this right of enforcement, all must have it. This means that each individual may use harmful or even deadly force to defend against invasions of his rights, to extract reparation from those who have violated his rights, and to punish violators of rights. Individuals are morally free to come to the defense of others and to help them extract reparations for harms done to them; and individuals may punish violators of the law of nature even if specific victims do not call for that punishment.

In explaining the right of defense and punishment, Locke occasionally uses language which suggests that the fundamental law of nature does direct individuals toward the maximization of human preservation. In the most striking instance of this language, Locke tells us that,

> . . . *the fundamental law of nature, man being to be preserved* as much as possible, when all cannot be preserved, the safety of the innocent is to be preferred: and one may destroy a man who makes war upon him, or has discovered an enmity to his being . . . (1980, II, 16)

In saying that mankind is *as much as possible* to be preserved, Locke suggests that the justification for using lethal force against a lethally minded attacker is that this deadly force will preserve more lives than would be preserved if that attacker were allowed to proceed with his lethal intent. Or the *policy* of using deadly force against lethally minded attackers is justified because it preserves more lives than would be preserved than under the *policy* of allowing lethally minded attackers to proceed.

Yet, if that were Locke's doctrine, he would have to say that, if two individuals set out to kill a single other person and both of those lethally minded attackers have to be killed in order to prevent the one murder, then the murder ought to be allowed. Or he would have to say that if a policy of allowing lethally minded killers to proceed would cost less lives than a policy of killing lethally minded attackers, the former policy should be adopted. Yet it is clear that Locke would not say either of these things. For what is crucial for Locke is the difference between the innocence of the intended victim and the guilt of the aspiring victimizer. The innocent are to be preferred not because there are more of them than there are attackers but, rather, because they are *innocent*. And the killing, if necessary, of the attackers is justified not because there are fewer of them but, rather, because they have taken themselves beyond the protection of the law of nature. Here is how the sentence fragment in Locke that I have cited immediately above continues,

> . . . for the same reason he [on whom war is being made] may kill a *wolf* or a *lion*; because such men [the aggressors] are not under the ties of the commonlaw of reason, have no other rule, but that of force and violence, and so may be treated as beasts of prey . . . (1980, II, 6)

Similarly, Locke tells us that,

> In transgressing the law of nature, the offender declares himself to live by another rule than that of *reason* and common equity. . . . and so he becomes dangerous to mankind, the tye, which is to secure them from injury and violence, being slighted and broken by him. Which being a trespass against the whole species . . . every man upon this score by the right he hath to preserve mankind in general, may restrain, or where it is necessary, destroy things noxious to them . . . (1980, II, 8)

The aggressor has "renounced reason" and engaged in "unjust violence and slaughter." He has declared himself not to live by reason and common equity and has become a danger to others. This, and not any calculation of how many lives will be preserved by alternative courses of action, is why the criminal "may be destroyed as a lion or a tyger . . ." (1980, II, 11).[2] Since there is a law of nature which governs the state of nature, there can be criminality and injustice in the state of nature. That is why, in the state of nature, men may *justly* respond with acts of defense, extraction of restitution, and punishment.

As we have just seen again, to say that men possess rights in the state of nature is not to say that those rights will always be respected. Rather, it is to say that there are natural moral principles that allow one to distinguish, even in the state of nature, between just and lawful and unjust and unlawful behavior. These principles are "as intelligible to a rational creature, and a studier of that law, as the positive [i.e., enacted] laws of common-wealths" and most individuals in the state of nature will have some disposition to abide by them—in part because most individuals will have reason to believe that most other individuals will have some disposition to abide by them. Thus, it is of practical as well as logical significance to spell out the difference between the state of nature and the state of war— a difference which "some men [especially Hobbes] have confounded."

The state of nature consists in the absence of "a common judge with authority," whereas the state of war consists in the use of "force without right" (1980, II, 19). Men in a state of nature may also be in a state of war. But they need not be. For men may desist from using force without right even in the absence of a common judge. Moreover, just as men in the state of nature need not be in a state of war, men in a political state—that is, men over whom there is a common power—may be in a state of war. The existence of a common power over men does not exclude the use of force without right. Indeed, that common power itself is likely to be the wielder of that unjust force. Hence, according to Locke, men cannot adequately protect themselves against being in a state of war by merely establishing a common power over themselves. They will need a special sort of common power—a common power which itself will be barred from using force without right.

That is certainly not the sort of common power that Hobbes offers. For the Hobbesian sovereign "may do to all his subjects whatever he pleases, without the least liberty to any one to question or controul those who execute his pleasure." Locke's view is that no individual endowed with reason and our inborn disposition to pursue happiness and self-preservation would ever choose such a regime over the state of nature.

> . . . much better it is in the state of nature [as Locke understands it] wherein men are not bound to submit to the unjust will of another: And if he that judges, judges amiss in his own, or any other case, he is answerable for it to the rest of mankind. (1980, II, 13)

As one should expect, Locke's distinction between the state of nature and the state of war incorporates crucial anti-Hobbesian premises— premises grounded in the arguments we have just surveyed. In the state of nature, without appeal to the will of any (earthly) ruler, we can differentiate between actions that are done with right and actions which are done without right, between actions which accord with justice and actions that violate justice. Moreover, even after an (earthly) ruler comes on the scene, we can continue to apply these natural principles of right and wrong and justice and injustice. Most strikingly, we can continue to apply those principles *to the ruler himself.* The ruler's will can easily be an "unjust will." Here we get Locke's steady and characteristic insistence that political rulers are always subject to the same fundamental moral principles that govern individuals in their interactions with one another.

> For where-ever violence is used, and injury done, though by hands appointed to administer justice, it is still violence and injury, however coloured with the name, pretences, or forms of Law . . . (1980, II, 20)

The Earth as Common to all Mankind

Locke uses "property" in both a broad and a narrow sense. In the broad sense, property is that which men possess with propriety, for example, "their lives, liberties, and estates" (1980, II, 123). When Locke says the fundamental purpose of government is the protection of people's property, he is using "property" in this broad sense. In the narrow sense, property is external possessions, that is, "estate" which one possesses with propriety. From the very start of the Second Treatise, each person's free disposition of his possessions is included within Locke's understanding of our natural and perfect freedom. When Locke states the conclusions of the perfect freedom, false presumption, and like reason arguments, each person's *possessions* are included among the objects to which that individual has rights. Yet Locke cannot mean that an individual's right to freedom is infringed whenever *anything* he possesses is destroyed or taken from him. For the thief's right to freedom is not violated when he is required to return the stolen goods to its owner. The thief's freedom does not include the liberty to dispose of *others'* rightful possessions as he sees fit. What Locke must mean when he says that the law of nature forbids depriving individuals of their possessions is that individuals may not be deprived of their *rightful* or *just* possessions. Locke must, therefore, provide an account of the rise of rightful private possession.

Locke begins his account of private property by acknowledging that he may have argued himself into a difficult corner (1980, II, 25). For, to counter Filmer's claim that God gave the earth to Adam, Locke repeatedly asserts that God has given the earth to all mankind in common. Yet it seems that if the earth belongs to all mankind in common, no individual may even use any portion of natural material without everyone first consenting to such private use. Moreover, Filmer has argued that all of mankind has never or will never enter into such a compact; and, strikingly, Locke accepts this point (1960, I, 87). Hence, Locke concludes that he must find a non-contractual basis for private property. As he puts it,

> I shall endeavor to shew, how men might come to a *property* in several parts of that which God gave to mankind in common, and that without any express compact of all the commoners. (1980, II, 25)

The first task within Locke's endeavor is to show that the original common ownership of the earth by all mankind *allows* individuals to use or appropriate portions of the earth "without express compact of all the commoners." Locke's argument here is that the original common ownership must allow the private use or appropriation of portions of the earth without the consent of all commoners precisely because such universal consent has never occurred and will never occur. Since that consent has never and will never occur, if such consent is necessary, all private use or appropriation would be morally forbidden and human beings could survive only through morally prohibited uses or appropriations of the earth. To avoid immorality, people would have to just sit still and starve. "If such a consent as that [i.e., a universal compact] was necessary, man had starved, notwithstanding the plenty God had given him" (1980, II, 28). Since it is absurd to think that morality requires that everyone just sit still and starve, the original common ownership to the earth cannot require that all individuals get universal consent for their use or appropriation of portions of nature.

The earth is originally the common possession of all mankind only in the sense that originally it is not the rightful possession of any particular man (or group of men). Speaking of the natural fruits of the earth and the beasts which feed on those fruits, Locke says that their belonging to mankind in common is a matter of "no body [having] originally a private dominion, exclusive of the rest of mankind, in any of them, as they are thus in their natural state . . ." (1980, II, 26). Locke argues to the same conclusion in the *First Treatise*. Rights with respect to nature must be consistent with the fact ". . . that Man should live and abide for some time upon the face of the Earth . . ." (1960, I, 86). The most fundamental natural liberty is the liberty of self-preservation; individuals cannot by nature be obligated to forego basic self-preserving activities. Hence, there can be no natural right that requires that men forego such activities. Since individuals must use and appropriate from nature if they are to preserve themselves, the liberty of each to preservation himself implies a liberty of each to use and appropriate from nature.

> Reason, *which was the Voice of God in him*, could not but teach him and assure him, that pursuing that natural Inclination he had to preserve his Being, he followed the Will of his Maker, and therefore had a right to make use of those Creatures, which by his Reason or Senses he could discover would be serviceable thereunto. And thus Man's *Property* in the Creatures was founded upon the right he had, to make use of those things, that were necessary or useful to his Being. (1960, I, 86)

Locke offers a nice example of how some material can be said to be commonly held without it following that each relevant agent must agree before either agent can use or appropriate some of that material. A father provides a chunk of meat to his children. Even though that chunk is "provided for them in common," any one of the children may cut herself a slice without first getting permission from all the other children. Indeed, that child may not merely "use" that slice but may appropriate it into her body (1980, II, 29).

So far Locke has only vindicated a liberty to use or appropriate, not a right *to* the appropriated or transformed object. He has vindicated Tom's using or appropriating some raw material; but he has not shown that John's making off with that material while Tom is taking a nap violates any right of Tom's. It is another step to establish "a Property in any particular thing" (1960, I, 87).

Rights over Permissibly Appropriated Objects

How, then, are we to get beyond mere permissible use and appropriation? Locke thinks that we *need* to get beyond mere permissible use and appropriation because, at least for the most part, men need *property* in what they are using or what they have appropriated if that use or appropriation is reliably to serve their ends. John needs to be able to count on that nicely shaped stone still being there when he comes back to his root pounding site. (Even if John is an employee of Robert, John's steady employment as a root pounder depends upon *Robert's* secure possession of the stone.) Since Locke believes that the natural moral order must be conducive to individual self-preservation—indeed to "comfortable preservation," (1960, I, 87)—he believes that this moral order must allow men to get beyond mere permissible use and appropriation. Still, he needs to explain *how* the further move to "a Property" in particular things takes place. Moreover, just as he has explained the permissibility of individuals making use of or appropriating portions of nature without appeal to a social compact, he now has to explain the emergence of property rights in permissibly appropriated material without appeal to a social compact.

The core of Locke's solution is to turn back to the right that each rational individual has over his own person which has been established in the *Second Treatise*'s opening chapters. Since every individual has by nature a proprietorship over himself, each individual has by nature a right to his our labor. As Locke puts it, ". . . every man has a *property* in his own *person*. This no body has any right to but himself. The *labour* of his body, and the *work* of his hands, we may say are properly his" (1980, II, 27). Locke's next premise is that in appropriating material from nature one mixes one's labor with or invests one's labor in that bit of material. Here appropriation is understood as purposeful; it is not merely a matter of some grains of sand sticking to one's feet as one walks along the beach. Such appropriation of material will necessarily transform that material in some way—even if only by moving the acorn from the ground to one's mouth. In many instances much more than the material's physical location will be changed through one's bringing one's efforts, energies, and skills to bear upon that material. The stone gets transformed into a spearhead. The branch gets transformed into a bow. The rock and stump infested field is cleared and readied for cultivation. Locke's third premise is that, when in such a purposive way one mixes one's labor with and transforms some natural material, one's labor is invested and not merely abandoned. Locke does not tell us precisely where the boundary is between investment and abandonment; and, of course, within any given society that boundary will in part be determined by what people are used to viewing as investment or abandonment. Nevertheless, there are more than enough intuitively clear cases for us to understand quite well and find perfectly plausible what Locke is thinking when he says that individuals can and do mix their labor with raw material in the sense of investing the material with their labor. If John has so mixed his labor with a bit of raw material—transforming, let us say, a branch into a nicely shaped and useful spear—the resulting spear embodies John's non-abandoned rightful held labor.

Hence, if Tom comes along and makes off with that spear, Tom violates John's retained right over that invested labor. Since Tom cannot make off with that spear without making off with John's invested labor, we naturally say that John has a right to the spear vis-a-vis Tom. Since John's right to his labor is a right he has against all other persons, the right to the spear that John acquires by way of mixing his labor with the branch is a right against all other persons. Each man has a right to the fruits of his labor because each has a right to that in which *his* workmanship is embodied.[3]

Recall that Locke's vindication of private property has two stages. First, he needs to show that individuals may use or appropriate portions of nature without their getting everyone's consent; second, he needs to show that actions which individuals may permissibly engage in will generate rights to particular extra-personal objects. An elegant feature of Locke's doctrine is the tight connection between (i) the uses or appropriations which an agent may permissibly perform because of his liberty of self-preservation and (ii) the uses or appropriations which generate rights for that agent. The tight connection is that they are the very same actions.

. . . . subduing or cultivating the earth, and having dominion, we see are joined together. The one gave title to the other. So that God, by commanding to subdue, gave authority so far to *appropriate*: and the condition of human life, which requires labour and materials to work on, necessarily introduces private possession. (1980, II, 35)

The very actions that must be permissible if men are to preserve themselves by making use of the earth *also* generate rights to the holdings which result from those actions.

This is a good point to emphasize five further points about Locke's theory of property.

***

First, the labor that Locke speaks of people mixing with natural material is to be understood very broadly. In the purposeful transformation of raw material individuals employ their energies, time, natural capacities, acquired skills, and insights about opportunities for transformations. In his purposeful transformation of raw material, an individual invests all those aspects of his person which constitute his *industriousness*. Locke tells us that labor includes "invention and arts" (1980, II, 43).

Second, Locke's own sense of what counts as property generating investment of labor may nevertheless be more narrow than it needs to be. Suppose a number of families or clans cooperate with one another to establish boundaries that define exclusive family or clan domains for the hunting of beavers. They do so because they sense that the establishment of such exclusive domains will prevent overhunting. Once such separate domains exist, the family or clan which limits its hunting today gets the benefit of more beavers available for it to hunt in the future.[4] Here is an exercise of industriousness which transforms the beaver hunting territory but not by itself physically changing that territory. The spirit of Locke's doctrine would, I believe, count the industriousness of the families or clans in developing, enforcing, and abiding by these boundaries as a property generating investment. Yet Locke is certainly not envisioning such modes of invested industriousness when he is writing the *Second Treatise*.

Third, Locke clearly envisions individuals exchanging and making donations of the fruits of their respective labors. Through voluntary contract Tom may acquire a right to the fruits of John's labors while John acquires a right to the fruits of Tom's labors. Probably because Locke is so confident that the law of nature includes the rights and obligations of agreements, he does not pursue any further explanation of why an individual to whom a voluntary transfer of property is made acquires rights to that object *against all the world* and not just against the person who transferred that object to him.

Fourth, among the property which one may exchange with another is one's own labor. Tom may sell his labor—or a certain amount of it—to John; and, in that case, the fruit of that labor is rightfully *John's*. This is why "the turfs my servant has cut" (1980, II, 28) are my property.

Fifth, Locke's account of property rights which arise through agents' investing their self-owned labor is part of Locke's state of nature theory. It is part of his account of what rights individuals are either born to or can come to possess in the absence of any sort of political authority. Of course, when Locke says that rights over external possessions can and do arise within the state of nature, he is not saying that these property rights will be acceptably secure within the state of nature. There may in fact be so much insecurity within the state of nature that individuals will have very little incentive to engage in property creating activities.

Perhaps individuals will extensively engage in property generating activities only in the presence of a (duly circumscribed!) protective authority. However, even when the operation of such a protective authority serves as a precondition of people engaging in extensive and elaborate property generating activities, the property rights which are created belong to the labor-investing individuals and not to the protective authority. Consider this example. The Magnificent Seven's protection of the Mexican villagers against the Banditos is a precondition of the villagers planting more and more kinds of crops. Nevertheless, the villagers' rights to those crops arise *from their production of those crops*—just as they would were neither the Banditos nor the Seven on the scene. Of course, *if* the villagers have agreed to pay the Seven for the protection which the Seven provide against the Banditos—which well they might—then the protectors would have rights to *that* payment. Nevertheless, the mere fact that the Seven provide security in the absence of which the villagers' would not have grown as much does not make the Seven partial owners of those crops. Similarly, the fact that the activity of a more conventional protective institution is a precondition for more extensive and elaborate property rights coming into existence does not make that institution a partial owner of those rights.

The Provisos and Their Satisfaction in the Pre-monetary Phase

Locke insists that his doctrine does not imply that "any one may engross as much as he will." The law of nature that lies behind rights to extra-personal possessions also places two limitations on the extent to which individuals may engross. The first and less significant proviso is that an individual does not have a right to continued possession of some fruit of his labor if that fruit will spoil in the course of his continued possession. Let us call this the "spoilage proviso." If John has brought home a leg of venison from the hunt but half of it will putrefy before he can consume it, John does that have a right to that half of the venison.[5] Locke even says that an individual who holds on while some resource spoils has "invaded his neighbor's share" and, for this, he is "liable to be punished" (1980, II, 37). Recall Locke's example of the father who puts a chunk of meat before his children. Neither child need get the other's permission before cutting a slice for herself. Nevertheless, there is something wrong with one of the children cutting off more than she can consume and simply letting the excess spoil. Perhaps the engrossing child is liable to punishment not because the other child has a property right in the meat that spoils but, rather, because the first child's retention of that excess meat illicitly prevents the second child's use or appropriation of it. This modest understanding of the proviso is supported by Locke's statement that, when a portion of a cultivator's crop is about to spoil in his field "notwithstanding his inclosure, [that portion of the crop] was still to be looked on as waste, and might be the possession of any other" (1980, II, 38). This spoilage proviso arises not so much from basic premises of Locke's theory as from his own subscription to a hardwork, waste not, want not ethos. According to this ethos, the natural world exists for man's comfortable, albeit hard-earned, preservation; hence, it does not exist merely to be spoiled or destroyed (1980, II, 31 and 38).

The second and more important proviso is that appropriating individuals must leave "enough and as good" natural material in common for others (1980, II, 27). Several converging considerations underlie this proviso. First, we have seen that Locke repeatedly says that originally the earth belongs to all mankind in common. He insists that this does not amount to any strong form of original joint ownership of the earth. Yet Locke may have the sense that there is something about this original common ownership which provides each individual with some sort of residual claim to access to materials to labor upon. Recall again the children who have been presented with the chunk of meat. Either may cut herself a slice without getting the other's permission; but there is something wrong with one child cutting so large a slice that not enough is left for the other—even if this slice is not too much for the cutter to consume.

Second, Locke holds that the development of private property rights must be "without prejudice to any body" (1980, II, 36). The acquisition of property rights by John and Tom must, in some significant sense, not make Charles worse off. Hence, speaking especially of early moments in the rise of private property and of why, during those moments, the enough and as good proviso is not violated, Locke says,

Nor was this *appropriation* of any parcel of *land*, by improving it, any prejudice to any other man, since there was still enough, and as good left, and more than the yet unprovided could use. So that, in effect, there was never the less left for others because of his inclosure for himself: for he that leaves as much as another can make use of, does as good as take nothing at all. (1980, II, 33)

Third, advocacy of the enough and as good proviso and subscription to the idea that no one can be obligated to abide by a structure of property rights which is disadvantageous to him (relative to the earth remaining a commons) may derive from the role played by the liberty of self-preservation within the justification of private property rights. Since the liberty to engage in self-preserving action is at the base of the case for private property rights, the structure of rights which arises from that base must not deny any individual the liberty to use or appropriate in ways that are necessary to his self-preservation. Hence, a proviso must be attached to those property rights that makes clear that these rights are not to be construed so as to deny that basal liberty of self-preservation.

How much has to be left by those first establishing private property rights for those who have not themselves established property rights? Locke's answer decidedly is *not* an equal amount. The enough and as good proviso allows John to encompass an enormous amount as his property—much more than is left for Tom—as long as enough material is left for Tom to labor upon in pursuit of his self-preservation. The considerations which underlie the proviso suggest that as much has to be left for Tom's use or appropriation as would be available for Tom's use or appropriation were all natural material left in common. Tom has no just complaint under the enough and as good proviso if others' establishment of property rights leaves Tom with as much opportunity to employ his efforts, energies, and talents in pursuit of his self-preservation as he would have were property rights not established. Only if Tom is left with less opportunity to employ his labor in pursuit of his self-preservation than he would have were property rights not established does he have a just complaint under the proviso. Were the proviso to grant more to the individual who has not himself labored to establish property rights, it would grant to that individual the fruits of the labor of the industrious.

He that had as good left for his improvement, as was already taken up, needed not complain, ought not to meddle with what was already improved by another's labour: if he did, it is plain he desired the benefit of another's pains, which he had no right to . . . (1980, II, 34)

Anyone who demands more than the level of opportunity to labor in pursuit of self-preservation than he would enjoy in a pre-property state of nature reveals the "Covetousness of the Quarrelsome and Contentious" (1980, II, 34).

With the introduction of money, mankind enters into a second phase of the state of nature. But, before turning to these dramatic developments, we need to see why, according to Locke, the property rights that arise within the pre-monetary phase are most unlikely to run afoul of either of the provisos. With respect to the spoilage proviso, Locke points out that it is simply foolish to hoard up more than one can make use of; since most men are not foolish, there will be very little hoarding of what one cannot use. Moreover, this limitation can be circumvented by bartering away one's most perishable possessions (e.g., that half of the venison leg) for others' less perishable possessions (e.g., their nuts). Still, the really interesting story concerns the reasons for why it is most unlikely that the enough and as good proviso will be violated. Certainly there is no problem in the first ages of the world; for at that time "men were in more danger to be lost, by wandering from their company, in the vast wilderness of the earth, than to be straitened for want of room to plant in" (1980, II, 36). Even when the world is more fully populated, the development of private property does not straiten men. For the development of private property amounts to mankind's shift from a hunter-gatherer existence to an agricultural existence; and vastly *less* land is needed to support a family that is engaged in agriculture than is needed to support a family engaged in hunter-gathering. Therefore,

> . . . he who appropriates land to himself by his labour, does not lessen, but increase the common stock of mankind: for the provisions serving to the support of humane life, produced by one acre of inclosed and cultivate land, are (to speak much within compass) ten times more than those which are yielded by an acre of land of an equal richness lying waste in common. [Locke quickly revises the ratio to one hundred to one] And therefore he that incloses land, and has a greater plenty of the conveniencies of life from ten acres, than he could have from an hundred left to Nature, may truly be said to give ninety acres to mankind. (1980, II, 37)

Suppose that the ratio is fifty to one. So 500 acres of uncultivated land are needed to support a hunter-gather family while 10 acres are needed to support an agricultural family, perhaps with "more plenty of the conveniencies of life." When one family withdraws from a band of 20 families who jointly need 10,000 acres, it does so by enclosing 10 of those acres. They thereby leave 9,990 acres in common for the rest or nearly 526 acres apiece. When a second family withdraws from the band, the amount of land in common per family within the band undergoes a similar increase. Beyond these benefits to those who still draw their livelihood from the commons, there is the benefit of trade with those who have enclosed portions of the earth and turned to agriculture. Inhabitants who themselves do not enclose may "think themselves beholden to him, who, by his Industry on neglected, and consequently waste Land, has increased the stock of Corn, which they wanted" (1980, II, 36). Finally, in the pre-monetary stage of the state of nature, individuals or families will enclose only as much land as will yield—either directly or through barter—as much in the way of perishables as will make for their comfortable preservation. In the pre-monetary stage individuals have no incentive to enclose beyond that point (1980, II, 48). Thus, in the pre-monetary stage of the state of nature, there will be a strong tendency for people to abide by both the spoilage and the enough and as good provisos.

Money and the Satisfaction of the Provisos in the Commercial Phase

Yet money does come into existence; and it comes into existence *within* the state of nature, hence, *not* because of any governmental action. Locke tells us that money comes into existence because "fancy or agreement" puts a value on nonperishable (and readily stored and transported) materials like gold and silver independent of the value that these materials have for "the necessary support of life" (1980, II, 46). Each of us has some fancy for glittery substances like silver and gold and, more than that, we each realize that everyone else has a similar fancy. Furthermore, some of these glittery substances—like gold and silver—are nonperishable, readily stored, easily transported, and their quantities can be measured with decent reliability. The result is that each of us knows that others will usually be willing to take certain quantities of these substances in exchange for materials that more directly provide "support for life." Through our mutual expectation that people will take gold and silver in

exchange for "really" useful goods, we each become even more willing
to take gold and silver in exchange—which makes others even more
willing to take gold and silver in exchange—and so on. This is the sense
in which "fancy" and "agreement" work together to generate the existence of money. Although Locke insists that money does not arise from
"compact," he does say that there is a sort of "tacit and voluntary consent" (1980, II, 50) to its existence. We shall see shortly why Locke wants
to say this.

The first and most obvious consequence of the appearance of money
is to deprive the spoilage proviso of any capacity to limit the extent of any
person's rightful wealth. All persons have to do is to make sure that their
wealth is in the form of gold or silver rather than putrefying venison. An
individual who exchanges his vast store of perishables for nonperishable
forms of money has

> . . . invaded not the right of others, he might heap up as much of the
> durable things as he pleased: the *exceeding of the bounds of his* just *prop-
> erty* not lying in the largeness of his possession, but the perishing of any
> thing uselessly in it. (1980, II, 46)

The second consequence of the appearance of money is that people
acquire enormous incentives to act in ways which at least *appear* to violate
the enough and as good proviso.

> Find out something that hath the use and value of money amongst his
> neighbours, you shall see the same man [i.e., the man who has only
> been producing to supply himself and his family] will begin presently
> to enlarge his possessions. (1980, II, 49)

For when people find themselves in position to engage in "commerce
with other parts of the world" and, therein, "to draw *money* to [them] by
the sale of the product" (1980, II, 48) they will radically increase the
extent of their production. And, often at least, that radical increase in
the extent of their production will involve a more extensive (and inten-
sive) use and appropriation of land and other natural materials. Even in
the pre-monetary state of nature men have "possessions in different pro-
portions" due to differences in the degree of their industry. The invention of money provides more industrious individuals with further
opportunities to enlarge their possessions; and this almost certainly will

generate greater inequality among men's holdings. The incentives to expand private holdings is sure to leave some individuals with less opportunity to use or appropriate raw materials than they would have were all the world still a commons. Thus, it seems that the invention of money leads to the violation of the enough and as good proviso.

Locke has a simple—albeit, superficial—first response to this. Some people being left without enough and as good raw materials to use or appropriate is an obvious outcome of the institution of money. Hence, since everyone has consented to the institution of money, everyone must have also agreed to this outcome. Thus, everyone has agreed to set aside the enough and as good proviso (1980, II, 50). Clearly this response is unsatisfactory. For one thing, it depends upon belief in the reality of universal consent; yet Locke himself has acknowledged that contentions within the theory of property cannot plausibly be supported by appeal to universal consent. It is true that Locke carefully says that in his vindication of private property he will avoid appeal to "express compact" and that in his account of money he says that money arises from "tacit" agreement. But if unsupported claims about tacit agreement are let in to explain the appearance of money, why shouldn't they be let in to vindicate private property rights? More importantly, Locke's initial response presses us to ask, *Why* would everyone consent to money if everyone sees that this will result in some having less opportunity to use or appropriate raw material? This question is especially pressing because Locke holds that no one enters into a contract except with an eye to advancing his own interests. Therefore, Locke must hold that the putative contract that leads to some having less opportunity to use or appropriate raw material than they would were all the earth still held in common is advantageous to everyone. Thus, we are lead to two more fundamental questions: Why does Locke believe that the introduction of money leads everyone to be better off than he would be were all the earth still held in common? How does the fact—if it is a fact—that the introduction of money would lead everyone to be better off support Locke's view that the enough and as good proviso is not (generally) violated in the monetary phase of the state of nature?

Locke thinks that everyone—or almost everyone—is made better off by the introduction of money despite the greater economic inequality which follows because of the immense incentives to productive activity which money creates. Part of Locke's picture here is that the prospect of hoarding up pieces of gold or silver leads people to produce more so that they will have products to exchange for more and more gold and silver (1980, II, 50). Yet Lockean agents are not primarily hoarders; they are pursuers of comfortable preservation, the conveniences of life, and happiness. What money does is to make commercial society (beyond mere barter) possible. The prospect of commerce through which an individual may "draw *money* to him by the sale of [his] product" (1980, II, 48) motivates the individual to create more and better products to sell primarily so that he will be able to purchase the more extensive and better products which others are producing primarily so that they will be able to purchase more and better products. This prospect of commerce—together with security in the fruits of one's labors and in the proceeds of one's exchanges—elicits an enormous increase in "human industry" (1980, II, 26). And human industry—that is, the exercise of human labor broadly understood—is the great source of economic value.

We have already seen Locke's claim that an acre employed in agriculture will be ten times—nay, one hundred times—more productive of the conveniences of life. Why? Because more or more specialized or more intelligent labor will be invested per cultivated acre than per hunting-gathering acre. Locke tells us that "it is labour indeed that puts the difference of value on everything." Speaking of the value of the products of the earth that are useful to the life of man, Locke repeats that "what in them is purely owing to *nature*, and what to *labour*, we shall find that in most of them ninety-nine hundredths are wholly to be put on the account of labour" (1980, II, 40). In contrast to the value generated by labor, "nature and the earth furnish only the almost worthless materials, as in themselves" (1980, II, 43). So we see that there is a double meaning to Locke's claim that labor is the great foundation of property. Labor is the foundation for persons' *rights* to property and labor is that which accounts for almost all of the *value* of the goods to which individuals have property rights. Yet these are two distinct doctrines. If, somehow, one's laboring on some raw material produced an object that was less valuable than the raw material had been, this would not undermine one's right to the resulting object. Also, one's labor may be the predominant factor in the production of some enormously valuable object, yet one will not have a right to that object if one's labor was under contract to another.

We should also guard against ascribing to Locke the labor theory of value according to which the economic value of any good is proportionate to the *amount* of labor that goes into its production. According to this labor theory of value, a certain number of units of labor are present in every productive action and the economic value of whatever is produced by a set of productive actions equals the total number of units of labor involved in that set of actions. Locke, to his credit, has no such notion of ultimate and commensurable units of labor; and he never says that the extent of the economic value of goods is a direct function of the number of the commensurate units of labor that go into its production. One further indication that Locke does not hold to the labor theory of value is his stance on the value of gold and silver. For, as we have seen, he holds that this value derives from fancy or agreement. Another indication is his statement that when land has significant value, that value arises from scarcity (1980, II, 45).

Locke is asserting the simple and correct proposition that the existence of economically valuable goods depends almost entirely upon the effort, energy, skill, and insight that human beings bring to their productive interaction with nature; in more recent terminology, it depends upon the development and exercise of human capital.[6] It is because of the predominant importance of human capital in the production of wealth that "numbers of men are to be preferred to largeness of domains" (1980, II, 42). This is why Locke favored the free movement of skilled labor into England from abroad.[7] This focus on the crucial importance of human industriousness is also why the "wise and godlike" prince is he who "by established laws of liberty [secures] protection and encouragement to the honest industry of mankind" (1980, II, 42).

How does all this connect with the enough and as good proviso? Locke's view is that the enormous increase in human industry which occurs under the laws of liberty and by way of the introduction of money, commerce, and the more elaborate forms of property and exchange which expanding commerce engenders is a rising tide which lifts all swimmers—or at least almost all the swimmers who are willing to swim with that tide. Locke's boldest statement of this rising tide thesis comes in a comparison he makes between the conveniences of life enjoyed by native Americans who have been liberally furnished with natural materials but (he thinks) have not at all caught the tide of commerce as Englishmen have.[8] The comparison is between the king of a large territory in America and a day-laborer in England; and Locke's striking claim is that this American king "feeds, lodges, and is clad worse than a day-labourer in *England*" (1980, II, 41). However, there are difficulties here. On the one hand, Locke's bold claim is far from obviously correct. On the other hand, this claim is more bold than Locke needs to make. In offering the king-day laborer comparison, Locke seems to be thinking that he has to show that the worst off individual in a monetary, commercial society is better off than the best off person in a pre-monetary, pre-commercial society. Yet, what he actually needs to show is considerably more modest than this.

Locke needs to show is that, for any given individual, the transition from pre-commercial society to commercial society is advantageous or at least not disadvantageous. (Hence, any given individual would be rational to agree to the introduction of money.) For each individual, the losses, if any, from the more extensive and aggressive privatization of raw material which occurs when money and widespread commerce arises has to be counterbalanced by the lift he receives from the rising tide of commerce. That lift may come in the form of more and more types of opportunity to work for the diverse sorts of enterprises which are expanded or created as people more and more develop and exercise their capacities for industry. Although in the monetary and commercial phase some individuals will not have enough and as good *in the way of natural materials* for them to use or appropriate, there is likely to be much more available to them to use or appropriate (via employment, rental, or purchase) than would have been available to them in the pre-monetary and pre-commercial phase. The lift may also come in the form of more and more types of conveniences available to the individual for purchase—perhaps at lower prices than under early barter arrangements. Locke does not have to hold that life goes swimmingly for everyone in the monetary and commercial phase—even for everyone who attempts to swim with that tide. Life at the close of the seventeenth century was inevitably *very* tough for most people. At most, he has to hold that the introduction of money and the rise of commercial society on net is advantageous to everyone (who is willing to adapt to it) or at least it is not disadvantageous.

Recall that Locke's official argument about the enough and as good proviso is that it is rescinded via people's mutual consent to money. Yet we raised the question of why people would rationally consent to money if its introduction leads to enough and as good raw materials *not* be left for everyone. We see now that Locke has a good answer to this question. The agreement is rational because, for each individual, the consequences of the introduction of money is *on net* advantageous (or at least not disadvantageous). Unfortunately, one major problem remains with the claim that this proviso is rescinded through rational mutual consent.

The problem is that this claim requires that there actually be universal agreement. Yet Locke is rightly skeptical of such claims about universal agreement. He is so skeptical that he explicitly sets out to give an account of private property that avoids appeal to universal agreement. Fortunately, there is another way for us to understand the significance for the proviso of Locke's claim about the mutual gains that arise through the emergence of private property and money.[9]

Let us go back to the liberty of self-preservation and the role it plays in Locke's doctrine of property. Suppose humans are still in the hunter-gather stage of their existence. All the raw material that is gathered or hunted or occupied is fairly immediately consumed as food, clothing, or places of abode; the only capital goods that are produced are primitive tools for hunting and gathering. At this stage, men's use and appropriation of extra-personal material is pretty much a zero-sum game. The effect of almost all use or appropriation by one party is to diminish the opportunity of others to use or appropriate. Insofar as nature replenishes itself, each annual cycle ushers in another zero-sum game. Under these conditions, each individual's moral liberty of self-preservation requires that some of this raw material—perhaps "enough and as good"—be left for him to labor upon. If human beings were to remain in the hunter-gatherer stage, the liberty of self-preservation would always require that enough and as good raw material be left for others; *and* because of the zero-sum feature of the hunter-gatherer game, this requirement would significantly restrict the extent of everyone's rightful use or appropriation.

However, human history involves a great escape from this zero-sum game. Human industry well beyond that involved in hunter-gathering is stimulated by the possibilities and actualities of private property and engagement in commerce. And human labor—which, recall, is the exercise of human energy, skill, and insight—dwarfs raw materials in its contribution to production. This human industry so radically increases opportunities for persons to bring their productive powers to bear on the world that the loss to any given individual in opportunity to use or appropriate *raw* materials is (very likely to be) overbalanced by gains in other opportunities to employ his productive powers. Hence, once the potentiality of human industry is released, the liberty of self-preservation does not require that enough and as good *raw* material be left for each. What each individual's liberty of self-preservation does continue to require is that this individual have as much opportunity to employ his productive powers as he would have had if all raw material had remained in common. However, the satisfaction of this ongoing enough and as good requirement never—or at least rarely—imposes any restriction on the extent of anyone's rightful possessions. On this reading of Locke, the enough and as good proviso is not rescinded. It remains true that no one is to be made to have less opportunity to bring his labor to bear on the world for the sake of his own ends than he would have were private property and money not introduced. However, once mankind escapes the hunter-gatherer stage, there is no reason to express this proviso specifically in terms of enough and as good *raw materials* being left. And once mankind enters the positive-sum world of "honest industry," there is good reason to think that this more generally understood proviso will (almost) always be satisfied.

Although this final understanding of Locke on the enough and as good proviso may not have been Locke's explicit understanding, it does nicely highlight Locke's belief that the route to increased material well-being for all lies in the establishment and the elaboration of private property and the expansion of markets and trade. One presupposition of this belief cannot be emphasized too much, viz., that mutual beneficial economic interaction is *possible*. Here is how Locke represents an individual seeking economic gain back in the early *ELN*:

> . . . when any man snatches for himself as much as he can, he takes away from another man's heap the amount he adds to his own, and it is impossible for anyone to grow rich except at the expense of some one else. . . . no gain falls to you which does not involve somebody else's loss. (1997, p.131)

In *ELN*, economic gain has nothing to do with labor, industry, or production; it is entirely a matter of *snatching* what someone else would otherwise have. One of the outstanding features of Locke's discussion of property in the *Second Treatise* is how thoroughly it breaks with this primitive zero-sum perspective.

The Enough and As Good Proviso and the Poor Law

I have ascribed to Locke the view that everyone (or almost everyone) gains in the transformation of human society from the hunter-gatherer stage to the pre-monetary private property stage and from the pre-monetary stage to the commercial stage. However, nothing in Locke's theory excludes the *possibility* that some individuals' opportunities to fend for themselves will be diminished by the generally beneficial process of privatization. Moreover, as Locke looks around the world of late seventeenth-century England, he sees plenty of people in dire straits. Those among them who are in dire straits because of the developed structure of property rights,[10] have just complaints on the basis of the more generally understood enough and as good proviso. In his 1697 *An Essay on the Poor Law* (1997, p.131), Locke advanced various proposals for governmental action to deal with the problem of people in dire straits. I want to conclude this chapter with a brief discussion of the extent to which Locke's proposals in that essay represent the application of his broadly understood enough and as good proviso.

In the "Poor Law" essay, Locke proposes a range of policies for particular groups of unhappily situated people—young children who cannot be supported by their parents, teenagers who have wandered away from their home parishes, able-bodied adults, and not so able-bodied adults. The basic response across all these different groups is that people who need work have to been given work *and* they have to accept work. That those who need work *must* accept work when it is offered runs very much against the general pro-liberty tenor of Locke's writing. It especially runs counter to Locke's assertions in *A Letter Concerning Toleration* that individuals should be free to make all sorts of economically foolish decisions (1983, p.34). How could Locke have thought that *requiring* the indigent to accept work was consistent with the claims of liberty? Locke's view in the *Poor Law* essay seems to be that it is simply a given that provision will be made for those in dire straits. "Everyone must have meat, drink, clothing, and firing. So much goes out of the stock of the kingdom, whether they work or no" (1997, p.189). However, society cannot afford this provision unless the recipients as much as possible share in the burden of providing it. The way for these recipients to share in that burden is for them to make as much of a contribution to their own maintenance as possible.[11] No doubt another non-liberal aspect of Locke's thought is also at work here. This is his tendency to think in terms of the importance of *national* wealth and of everyone being obligated to contribute to national wealth by contributing whatever labor he can.

Let us put aside the requirement that those offered work must accept it and focus on the prior notion, viz., what is owed to those who are in dire straits is an opportunity to work. This seems to be precisely the response for which the generally construed enough and as good proviso calls. This aspect of Locke's thought is nicely expressed when he tells us that "the true and proper relief of the poor . . . consists in finding work for them." Locke's insistence that this relief not be at the expense of the just rights of others and also his hardwork, nose-to-the-grindstone ethic is expressed when he goes on to say " . . . and taking care they do not live like drones upon the labour of others" (1997, p.189).

4

From the State of Nature to the State

From the very beginning of the *Second Treatise*, Locke tells us that there are inconveniences in the state of nature and that the purpose of civil government is to remedy those inconveniences. In the central chapters of that *Treatise*, Locke provides an account of those inconveniences, of the sort of government that will remedy them and, hence, of what the true end of political authority is. He also attempts to identify the consent through which that political authority attains legitimacy.

The Inconveniences of the State of Nature and the Resigning Up of Rights

As has been noted, Locke is not entirely consistent in his depictions of the state of nature. When he is employing the state of nature to identify which rights individuals possess independent of governmental decree, Locke does not mention how insecure those rights may be in the absence of political authority. However, when he is employing the state of nature as part of a historical account of why people have moved quickly from that state to one of political governance, Locke puts a lot of emphasis on insecurity. Although in the state of nature each is ". . . absolute lord of his own person and possessions . . . yet the enjoyment of [this right] is very uncertain, and constantly exposed to the invasion of others." This is because "the greater part" of men are "no strict observers of equity and justice." The result is that the state of nature is "full of fears and continual dangers." This leads men to join in society "for the mutual *preservation* of their lives, liberties and estates, which I call by the general name, *property*" (1980, II, 123).

We have seen that in the state of nature each individual has the second-order right to act as an executor of the law of nature. Each may defend against invasive actions, each may extract restitution from violators of rights, and each may punish violators of rights. According to Locke, the insecurities of the state of nature do not arise from people's exercise or enjoyment of their first-order rights to life, liberty, estate, and fulfillment of agreements. Rather those insecurities arise through people's exercise of their second-order rights as executors of the law of nature, that is, each individual's reliance on his own private judgments about whether some first-order right has been violated, about what the acceptable level of reparation or punishment is for such a violation, and about who is guilty of the violation. Individuals will be biased on their own behalf when determining whether they have been wronged or have wronged others, what they may demand in reparations if they have been injured or what they must pay in reparation if they have injured, and how much they may punish if they have been wronged or how much they may be punished if they have wronged. Conflict is almost certain to ensue when these private judgments come into play.

Actually, according to Locke, inconveniences are rare in the early, that is, pre-monetary, stage of the state of nature; they only become frequent and troublesome with the introduction of money and the commercial society to which money gives rise. Before the invention of money, men's estates were relatively equal, simple, and stable. Tom had these 10 acres as an inheritance from his father and John had these 15 adjoining acres as an inheritance from his father; and for at least two generations, the stream that runs between these holdings has been recognized by all the potential jurors in the area as the boundary between their property. If Tom starts harvesting some berries growing on a bush on John's side of the stream, there will be little room for reasonable disagreement about whether this is an intrusion upon John's property rights. Moreover, Tom will have little incentive to invent clever arguments why he really has a right to harvest from that bush given how perishable those berries are and to how few people he can barter them:

> The equality of a simple poor way of living, confining their desires within the narrow bounds of each man's small property, made few controversies, and so no need of many laws to decide them, or variety of officers to superintend the process, or look after the execution of justice, where there were but few trespasses, and few offenders. (1980, II, 107) [1]

Things get more complicated and potentially contentious when those extra berries can be sold for pieces of silver to Charles who produces berry preserves "to draw money to him by the sale of the product" (1980, II, 48). Things get even more complicated, when John decides to use the flow of the stream to power a mill to grind the wheat which his neighbor Henriette uses in her bakery and this use diminishes the flow of water from the stream into Tom's irrigation ditch. As more uses and more valuable uses are discovered for raw materials and produced objects— which is the great boon to come from the introduction of money—the more incentive individuals will have to be disputatious about where the boundaries between their estates lie.

What is wanting in the state of nature—especially in its later, commercial phase—is an established common system for the enforcement of the law of nature, that is, for the protection of a person's first-order rights. More specifically, three conditions are absent in the state of nature: first, "an *established*, settled, known *law*, received and allowed by common consent to be the standard of right and wrong"; second, "*a known and indifferent judge*, with the authority to determine all differences according to the established law"; and third, a "*power* to back and support the sentence when right, and to *give* it due *execution*" (1980, II, 126). Hence, the natural avenue for escape from the state of nature is for individuals to transfer their second-order rights to a single shared agent who will have the right and duty to act as executor of the law of nature on behalf of each of those individuals. Through their authorization of this agent as their common executor of the law of nature, individuals bind themselves to comply with the system that agent creates for identifying what counts as a violation of persons' first-order rights, what reparation or punishment is due when some such violation occurs, who is liable for such reparation or punishment. For Locke, the agent to whom individuals transfer their original rights to act as executors of the law of nature is not any individual who exists prior to that transfer. Rather the transfer itself creates a new agent, which Locke refers to as "political society," "community," "common-wealth," or "civil society."

It is this new, more than moderately mysterious being, in whom the right and duty of exercising that law of nature is now vested. Political society in turn establishes an actual government with a determinate structure and particular officials charged with specific tasks. Corresponding to the three conditions which are needed, but absent, in the state of nature, the government that political society establishes will consist of a legislature to provide established, settled law, a judiciary of known and impartial judges to apply the law to particular cases, and an executive to enforce the law. Locke believes that political society within England had

sensibly established a constitutional structure in which legislative authority is shared by an elected house, a hereditary house, and the monarch,
and executive authority is held by the monarch. Moreover, political
society entrusts various individuals to occupy places within this constitutional structure and to employ their delegated powers for the sake of the
purpose for which political society and government has been created.
According to Locke, something further takes place in the course of the
creation of political society. Each party who transfers his second-order
rights also gives "a right to the common-wealth to employ his force, for
the execution of the judgments of the common-wealth, whenever he
shall be called to it" (1980, II, 88).[2] More broadly, each of these individuals agrees to be taxed in kind or in cash to provide to the government the
means needed to carry out its assigned functions. However, even one's
representatives may not impose on one taxation that is out of proportion
to the share of protection which one receives (1980, II, 140).

It is crucial to emphasize that, as Locke sees it, individuals create political authority through their transfer of their rights to act as executors of
the state of nature[3] and not through their resignation or transfer of their
first-order rights over their persons, liberties, and possessions. The purpose of the creation of political authority is the better protection of those
first-order rights—which stand outside of and serve as a measure of the
proper conduct of political authority. Hence, the political authority that
Locke envisions as the solution to the inconveniences of the state of
nature is inherently and quite radically limited. Locke provides two reasons why rational men seeking to escape from the state of nature would
never opt for an absolute sovereignty in which unlimited legislative, judicial, and executive authority all resided in the same man (or assembly).

The first reason is that such a regime would leave the sovereign in a
state of nature vis-a-vis each of his subjects. For the sovereign himself (or
itself) would not be subject to law; for that sovereign everything would be
legally permissible. But this raises a question about Locke's own scheme.
How would the legislative body within Locke's own tripartite constitutional system be subject to the law which it enacts? Locke can point out
that these legislators will continue to be subject to the law of nature
which, for example, requires that they not "dispose of the estates of the
subject *arbitrarily*, or take any part of them at pleasure" (1980, II, 138).
However, Locke wants also to say that under his scheme of government,
the legislators will be as much subject to the law that they *enact* as anyone
else in the realm. When legislation is placed in "collective bodies of men
. . . every single person [becomes] subject, equally with other the meanest

men, to those laws, which he himself, as part of the legislative, have established" (1980, II, 94). As Locke sees it, this is because the legislators are *also* subjects; they are subjects when they are not busy legislating and they are subjects when they are replaced as legislators by other subjects. Arbitrary rule

> . . . is not much to be feared in governments where the *legislative* consists, wholly or in part, in assemblies which are variable, whose members upon the dissolution of the assembly, are subjects under the common laws of their country, equally with the rest. (1980, II, 138)
> . . . in well-ordered common-wealths . . . the *legislative* power is put into the hands of divers persons, who duly assembled, have by themselves, or jointly with others, a power to make laws, which when they have done, being separated again, they are themselves subject to the law they have made; which is a new and near tie upon them, to take care, that they make them for the public good. (1980, II, 143)

Unfortunately for Locke, this is not much of a solution. Legislators, it seems, can easily insulate themselves from the harmful consequences of their own legislation by arranging for the benefits of legislation to accrue to themselves and their friends and the costs to fall upon others. Alternatively, legislators may mandate rules of conduct to which they are quite happy to be subject even though others will find their subjection to be burdensome and tyrannical. For instance, Anglican legislators may be quite content to live under their mandate that all subjects attend the Anglican church while non-Anglican subjects find that requirement quite chaffing. Placing legislation in "collective bodies of men" seems to do very little, if anything, to limit the legal powers of the legislators.[4]

Locke offers a second reason why individuals exiting the state of nature will not opt for an absolute sovereignty—in a single man or in an assembly. The reason is that to institute any such absolute sovereignty would be

> . . . to put themselves into a worse condition than the state of nature, wherein they had a liberty to defend their right against the injuries of others, and were upon equal terms of force to maintain it . . . (1980, II, 137)

In another shot at Hobbes, Locke asserts that to think that men would trade the state of nature for subjection to an absolute sovereign is, " . . . to think, that men are so foolish, that they take care to avoid what mischiefs may be done them by *pole-cats*, or *foxes*; but are content, nay, think it safety, to be devoured by *lions*" (1980, II, 93). And, Locke insists, political lions will act like lions. Anyone who thinks ". . . that *absolute power purifies men's blood*, and corrects the baseness of human nature, need read but the history of this, or any other age, to be convinced of the contrary" (1980, II, 92). Given the necessity of freedom for one's self-preservation and one's happiness, no rational man would engage in the surrender of rights that Hobbes depicts.

Locke tells us that "any number of men" (1980, II, 89) can form a political community; "because it injures not the freedom of the rest; as they are left as they were in the liberty of the state of nature" (1980, II, 95). Perhaps over time additional individuals, seeing the benefits of escape from the state of nature, will join in. This is Locke's response to Filmer's argument that, if men are naturally free, only universal consent could establish legitimate political authority. Just as Filmer was wrong in thinking that, if men are naturally free, universal consent is needed to establish private property, so too is he wrong to think that, if men are in that original state, legitimate political authority requires *universal* consent. Individuals may proceed to establish private property *and* to establish political society without universal consent because in neither case are third parties harmed. Locke also has a cute answer to the question of why there is no written evidence for original (nonuniversal) social compacts. His answer is that the advantages of civil society were recognized so early in human history that these original unions took place long before mankind had learned to keep records. " . . . letters seldom come in amongst a people till a long continuation of civil society has, by other more necessary arts, provided for their safety, ease, and plenty" (1980, II, 101). Moreover, in the early stages of human history, it did not occur to individuals or the simple political societies they had formed to create complex constitutional structures for their governance. For in these early stages, there were few conflicts within society and, hence, rulers were needed only to command the members of that society in warfare. Such rulers had absolute authority in war but enjoyed "a very moderate sovereignty" (1980, II, 108) at home. However, as society grows more wealthy and complex, not only does the need for an impartial umpire grow, so too does the temptation for rulers to seek luxury at the expense of their subjects. This is what makes it necessary for men of later ages ". . . to examine more carefully *the original* and rights *of government*; and to find out ways to *restrain the exorbitances*, and *present the abuses* of that power . . ." (1980, II, p.111).

Majoritarianism—Radically Constrained

According to Locke, when individuals form a political society they all agree to be bound by the will of their majority ". . . unless they expressly agreed in any number greater than the majority" (1980, II, 99). The whole point of forming political society is to avoid the conflict which arises when each individual forms and stands by his own private judgment about what actions call for restitution or punishment and to what extent. So a single common judgment must come out of the casting of votes among the membership; and the default rule for identifying such a common judgment is to see which proposed action receives majority support. Here we are speaking of decisions made by political society about precisely what governmental structure is to be established. However, the same reasoning applies within the established legislative bodies. Some rule for identifying the common judgment on a given issue has to be put into play; and unless some other rule is expressly chosen, it is reasonable to take majority rule to be the one which is in effect. Still, it is crucial to recognize Locke's tight restriction on the scope of majority rule.

As we have noted, in entering political society, individuals surrender only their second-order rights to defend against violations of rights, to extract reparations and to inflict penalties for the violation of rights. They do not surrender their first-order rights to life, liberty, and estate. Indeed, Locke says repeatedly, that their purpose in uniting their rights to act as executors of the law of nature is to better secure and protect their individual lives, liberties, and estates (1980, II, 131). Men surrender to the majority only the power that is "necessary to the ends for which they unite into society" (1980, II, 99). Locke reinforces this stance through his insistence that no individuals *can* hand over power over his live or liberty or over the lives, liberties or estates of others because ". . . no body has an absolute arbitrary power over himself, or over any other, to destroy his own life, or take away the life or property of another . . ." (1980, II, 135). Thus, the fundamental rights of the law of nature that morally restrict how individuals may behave toward one another in the state of nature remain fully in place after the creation of political society both as restrictions on how individuals may behave toward others *and* as restrictions on how political society and any government it establishes may behave toward individuals. In another of the most striking passages of the *Second Treatise*, Locke declares,

> The obligations of the law of nature cease not in society, but only in many cases are drawn closer, and have by human laws know penalties annexed to them, to inforce their observance. Thus the law of nature stands as an eternal rule to all men, legislators as well as others. (1980, II, 135)

The law of nature does not provide one specific and indisputable answer to every question about whether some action violates the rights of another. Does Tom's startling John by making a loud and unexpected sound constitute a violation of John's rights? Does John's diminishing the flow of water into Tom's irrigation ditch from the stream which divides their fields violate Tom's rights? Reasonable judgment can differ on these matters; but some common, public judgment is needed. It is the job of the legislature to form determinate and reasonable judgments about precisely where the boundary lines are which define what is John's and what is Tom's. In some cases, the law of nature will not leave much, if any, leeway for different reasonable judgments—for example, in the case of Tom's striking a non-consenting John in the head with a sledge-hammer. In other cases—like the water flow case—the law of nature by itself may say little about where the boundary lines should be drawn. In such cases, the key constraint on the legislature is that it draw lines which contribute to there being a clear and consistent system of property rights and that it not draw lines for the purpose of advancing one party's interest at the expense of another's.[5] There also may be reasonable disputes about what degree of punishment is appropriate for actions which are reasonably declared to be in violate of the law of nature. A further role for legislators is to settle upon a set of reasonable penalties that will be publically known as the penalties attaching to the violation of known laws.

The role of legislation is to remove various indeterminacies within the law of nature and, by doing so, to enable individuals to live with one another as though the law of nature contained no such indeterminacies. Individuals join society so that ". . . they may have the united strength of the whole of society to secure and defend their properties, and may have *standing rules* to bound it, by which every one may know what is his" (1980, II, 136). They join society "to preserve their lives, liberties, and fortunes, and by *stated rules* of right and property to secure their peace and quiet" (1980, II, 137). These stated rules are for "the regulating of *property* between the subjects one amongst the other . . . ." Yet this regulation is not to be understood as a power in the government "to take to themselves the whole, or any part of the subjects' *property*, without their own consent" (1980, II, 139). As Locke tells us in his early "An Essay on Toleration," the end of erecting government is only "to preserve men in this world from the fraud and violence of another" and "what was the end of erecting of government ought alone to be the measure of its proceeding." "[T]he good, preservation, and peace of men in [their] society . . . is and ought to be the standard and measure according to which [the legislator] ought to square and proportion his laws, and model and frame his government" (1997, p.135).

We should look at one further arena in which Locke is concerned to build fences around the exercise of political power—the domain of executive prerogative. This is the right or power of the executive—typically, the monarch—to act on his own discretion either in ways that are not legally required or even in ways that run counter to the letter of the established law. Friends of political authority often insist on the necessity for an expansive executive prerogative on the grounds that only the executive has the vision and interest to see what the public good is and what actions must be taken to promote that good. This was, indeed, one of the main arguments made by Charles I and his supporters in the 1630s and 1640s to justify his imposition of new taxes and forced loans. Locke accepts the idea that the executive ought sometimes to act at his discretion even in ways that run contrary to the written law. However, most of his examples involve the monarch *declining* to enforce a statute that will do harm if it is enforced with "inflexible rigour" (1980, II, 160). Moreover, Locke insists that legitimate executive prerogative must serve the public good; it may not serve any "distinct and separate interest from the good of the community" (1980, II, 163). There is a constant danger of executive prerogative being misused. So the people must continuously monitor its exercise. This raises the ever-recurring question of who shall be the judge? Locke's answer is that

. . . where the body of the people, or any single man, is deprived of their right, or is under the exercise of a power without right, and have no appeal on earth [i.e., no appeal to a common and impartial judge], then they have a liberty to appeal to heaven [i.e., to resist with force that deprivation of their right]. (1980, II, 168)

They are vindicated in doing so "by a law antecedent and paramount to all positive laws of men" which reserves that "ultimate determination to themselves . . ." (1980, II, 168). Locke offers one further example of the legitimate exercise of executive prerogative that needs to be discussed because it takes us back to questions about how we are to understand the fundamental law of nature. In the example, we have a fire that is about to spread to a house and, if that house catches fire, the fire will spread further (to one or more additional houses). Locke says that, in his exercise of his prerogative, the executive may order that this conductive house be pulled down before it catches fire. This will be a *justified* exercise of that prerogative because of the fundamental law of nature and government, viz., "That as much as may be, *all* the members of the society are to be preserved" (1980, II, 159). So here Locke seems to be saying that the fundamental law of nature directs the executive to impose losses on some if this will prevent greater losses for others. This appears to support the "utilitarian" understanding of the fundamental law and to conflict with the defense of rights understanding which I pressed in Chapter 2.

In fact, however, Locke's stance in the burning house case does not support the utilitarian understanding. First, Locke does not say that pulling down the conductive house is justified because *more* housing would be saved than destroyed through that action. Perhaps only one further (and smaller) house will be saved and yet the executive would be justified in pulling down the (larger) conductive house *to prevent it from conducting the fire* to that further house. Perhaps what vindicates pulling down the conductive house is not that more housing gets saved but, rather, that this house is about to serve as a conduit for the fire to move on to another's house. To sharpen the point, imagine that instead of a conductive house, there is a conductive fuse which, let us say, belongs to Tom. The fire is approaching one end of that fuse and at the other end is John's much short piece of fuse. An executive devoted to the defense of individual property rights could well reason that he may tear up Tom's fuse to prevent its conducting the fire to John's fuse. The vindication of tearing up Tom's fuse would not turn on whose fuse is bigger. Rather, to put it inexactly but vividly, it would be based on whose fuse is the aggressor fuse and whose fuse is the innocent fuse! To put it more exactly but less vividly, the exerciser of executive prerogative may destroy Tom's property because what is about to happen to that property is about to destroy John's property.

Although this, I think, is the main reason why we should not read Locke's judgment in the burning house case as supporting the utilitarian reading of the fundamental law, there is one further reason for this. The conductive house is going to burn anyway. For that reason, pulling it down is quite different from the standard case of imposing a loss on one party in order to prevent a greater loss being suffered by another party. In a standard case Charles' smaller house *which is not at all endangered by the fire* would be pulled down in order to save John's larger house from the fire. Perhaps pulling down poor Charles' house will provide the material out of which fire fighting equipment can be quickly constructed to suppress the fire before it reaches John's house. Endorsing, as Locke does, the pulling down of Tom's conductive house (*which will burn anyway*) in order to save John's house is a long way from endorsing in utilitarian fashion the pulling down of Charles' house (which is safely distant from the fire) in order to save John's house. So we have two good reasons against taking Locke's endorsement of the destruction of the *conductive* and *doomed* house as a sign that he has a utilitarian understanding of the maxim that mankind is to be preserved as much as possible.

The Doctrine of Consent

Still, crucial questions remain about how *precisely* individuals resign up their rights and make themselves subject to political authority and about how *many* individuals in a given territory have actually gone through this process and are, thereby, actually subject to political authority. Even though any number of men can create a political society, Locke is eager to conclude that every adult individual[6] living in England in 1689 had somehow *through consent* become subject to the just established laws of England. As we shall see, to reach this conclusion Locke has to advance some pretty desperate contentions about the nature of authorizing consent.

Locke offers two distinctions that are intended to play an illuminating role in his doctrine of consent. The first is between consent which makes one *a member of political society* and consent which merely makes one *subject to the law* of the government which reigns over the territory in which one resides. The second distinction is between *express* and *tacit* consent. It is natural to think that Locke's view is that express consent and only express consent makes an individual a member of society (and, by implication, subject to the law) while tacit consent and only tacit consent *merely* makes one subject to the law. However, Locke's actual position is more complicated and more confused than this. The confusion stems from the fact that Locke really has two different notions of membership in political society. One of these is linked to one's inheritance of land that has become permanently associated with a given political society; the other notion is linked to "actual agreement" to and "express declaration" of one's membership.

Locke begins his sustained account of consent by postulating that whenever a landowner becomes a member of political society that individual annexes a clause to his will which requires that any heir to that land also become a member of that political society. A father cannot through *his own* consent bind his son to any political society. But a father may, ". . . annex such conditions to the land, he enjoyed as a subject of any common-wealth, as may oblige his son to be of that community, if he will enjoy those possessions which were his father's . . ." (1980, II, 116). To inherit the land of his father, the son must take the land "under the same terms his father did, by becoming a member of the society" (1980, II, 117). Presumably, the annexed clause also requires any subsequent *purchaser* of the land to become a member of the political society— although it is striking that it does not occur to Locke to add this stipulation. (One assumes that the reason that we have no written evidence of these clauses is that, like the original agreement that first created political society, these clauses were composed before the invention of writing!) However, Locke also seems to hold that individuals who are members of political society in virtue of their land ownership can quit that political society by divesting themselves of the land.

> . . . whenever the owner, who has given nothing but such a *tacit consent* to government will, by donation, sale, or otherwise, quit the said possession, he is at liberty to go and incorporate himself into any other common-wealth; or to agree with others to begin a new one . . . (1980, II, 121)

In virtue of the annexed clause, current ownership of land which itself is tied to the political society makes one a member of political society—even though this form of membership does not derive from express consent. And, if this is one's form of membership, one can dissolve one's membership by terminating one's ownership of the relevant land.

In contrast, if one's membership in political society arises from express consent, one cannot by one's choice dissolve that membership.

> . . . he, that has once, by actual agreement, and any *express* declaration, given his *consent* to any common-wealth, is perpetually and indispensibly obliged to be, and remain unalterably a subject to it, and can never be again in the liberty of the state of nature; unless, by any calamity, the government he was under comes to be dissolved; or else by some public act cuts him off from being any longer a member of it. (1980, II, 121)

If one has become a member of political society by way of express declaration, one's membership will be terminated only if the government which that society has created is destroyed or if that society expels one. To be such a "a member of that society" is to be "a perpetual subject of that common-wealth."

There is no reason not to allow Locke two kinds of membership in political society—the kind that arises from the inheritance (or, one presumes, purchase) of land to which an entangling clause has been annexed and which can be terminated by the owner through his sale or donation of that land and the kind that arises from express declaration and which cannot be terminated by the will of the member. To embrace both kinds of membership, Locke need only restrict his claim that one cannot be a member of political society without being "a perpetual subject of that commonwealth" to those who are members of political society *by way of express declaration.*[7] Moreover, we can readily allow that all members of political society are by implication subject to the enacted laws of that society. Nevertheless, it is clear that only a pretty small percentage of the individuals who Locke wants to say are subject to the enacted law are members of political society. Hence, Locke has to cast a much wider net to explain how all these other individuals are also subject to the law. That wider net is all the tacit consent which goes on beyond the tacit consent of those who inherit (or purchase) estates. To haul all these other individuals in, Locke tells us that

> . . . every man, that hath any possessions, or enjoyment, of any part of the dominions of any government, doth thereby give his *tacit consent,*

and is as far forth obliged to obedience to the laws of that government, during such enjoyment, as any one under it; whether this his possession be of land, to him and his heirs for ever, or a lodging only for a week; or whether it be barely travelling freely on the highway; in effect, *it reaches as far as the very being of any one within the territories* of that government. (1980, II, 119)

This solves the problem of not enough individuals giving their consent by making it almost impossible for anyone not to give his consent. If enjoyment of anything while living within the territory of a given government constitutes tacit consent to that government and thereby generates an obligation to obey its laws, then almost every individual living under almost every government which has ever existed or will ever exist has tacitly or will tacitly consent to that government and thereby has been or will be obligated to obey the laws of that government.

This is a theoretically disastrous outcome for Locke. For Locke wants the demand that regimes have the consent of the governed to have some real cutting force. He wants to be able to point to lots of regimes whose enacted law may generally be resisted precisely because those regimes do not have the consent of the governed. Yet, on Locke's explication of tacit consent, at least almost all *criminal* regimes will count as having the consent of at least almost all of the governed. As Filmer anticipated in his critique of consent theory, from any such appeal to tacit consent, "it follows that every prince that comes to a crown, either by succession, conquest or usurpation, may be said to be elected by the people" (1991, p.21) Another problem for Locke arises from the fact that only a small percentage of the governed count as members of political society. For Locke has told us that it is in the course of becoming a member of political society that individuals give their consent to be subject to taxation. It follows then that only a small percentage of the governed will legitimately be subject to taxation. (If the cost of becoming a member of political society includes the cost of becoming subject to taxation, even fewer people will choose to perform whatever actions would make them members of political society.)

Let us close this discussion by noting one possible route by which Locke may be able to escape from heavy reliance upon such a questionable doctrine of consent. Locke tells us that tacitly consenting individuals are as obligated to obey the government's laws "as any one under it" (1980, II, 119), "as far forth as any subject of it" (1980, II, 120), or "as far forth as any denison" (1980, II, 122). How far forth is that? People's basic natural law obligations are to abstain from invading the lives, liberties, and estates of others (and to abide by the enough and as good proviso). Justifiable enacted laws more specifically define and delineate persons' rights of life, liberty, and estate, attach known penalties to the violation of those rights, and enforce those penalties so that the disputes over rights and the insecurity of rights which plague the state of nature are overcome. Does one need to agree or consent to obey such enacted laws in order to be obligated to do so? The answer seems to be, no. The obligation to abide by such enacted laws no more depends upon one's agreement than does the obligation in the state of nature not to torture innocent children for the fun of it. If enacted law genuinely results in the obligations of the law of nature being "drawn closer, and hav[ing] by human laws know penalties annexed to them, to inforce their observation" (1980, II, 135), the obligation to observe that enacted law simply does not seem to require consent. Here, however, is the exception. Consent is necessary to obligate one to submit to enacted taxation. For in the state of nature there is no obligation to surrender portions of one's property to anyone—even if that party proclaims that the surrendered resources will be used for one's protection. If, in a state of nature or of society, others may permissibly take my possessions without my consent, those possessions are not my property.

> . . . for I have truly no *property* in that, which another can by right take from me, when he pleases, against my consent . . . a man's *property* is not at all secure, tho' there be good and equitable laws to set the bounds of it between him and his fellow subjects, if he who commands those subjects have power to take from any private man, what part he pleases of his *property*, and use and dispose of it as he thinks good. (1980, II, 138)

Although Locke takes people's consent to taxation to be an addendum to their consent to be members of political society or to be subject to the law, that consent to taxation may turn out to be the core claim on the basis of which the legitimacy of the constrained Lockean state rests.

5

Conquest, Resistance, and Dissolution

The last four chapters of the *Second Treatise*, "Of Conquest," "Of Usurpation," "Of Tyranny," and "Of the Dissolution of Government," are devoted to the conditions under which forcible resistance to existing political rulers is justifiable. That doctrine of justified resistance is grounded in and emerges from the law of nature theory which Locke expounds in the opening five chapters of the *Second Treatise* and the theory of the purpose, duties, and limits of government which he develops in the middle chapters of that work. We shall note deficiencies within Locke's doctrine of justified resistance that reflect problems within his doctrine of consent. We should always keep in mind that the *Two Treatises* were not written merely as an academic exercise; rather they were composed as a critique of ideological defenses of an actually existing authoritarian regime and as an intellectual defense of actually intended revolutionary activities. Richard Ashcraft (1986) does an impressive job of connecting the examples Locke offers of acts by political rulers whereby they forfeit their right to rule to the actual efforts of Charles II and James II to secure and expand their power.

Conquest and Usurpation

Locke's chapters on conquest and usurpation (wrongful seizure of governmental power) are less directly connected to political events within England in Locke's lifetime than are the chapters on tyranny and the dissolution of government. For neither Charles II nor James II were conquerors or usurpers. Nevertheless, the chapter "Of Conquest" is of considerable interest. For this chapter is a general critique of the view that legitimate political authority can arise through conquest. Although it does not speak directly to Englishmen about their situation, it does come to the conclusion that "the Grecian christians" of Locke's day "may justly cast off the Turkish yoke" (1980, II, 192). According to Locke, men from different nations are in a state of nature with respect to one another. This does not mean that anything which men from one nation may do to men from another is permissible or lawful. For, as we know, the state of nature has a law of nature to govern it. That law forbids aggressive attacks, that is, uses of force without right; and it fully allows defensive attacks and the forcible extraction of reparations or imposition of punishments upon aggressive attackers. If the King of Denmark were to attack England aggressively and conquer it, he would be an unjust conqueror. If, on the other hand, the King of Denmark were to respond to attacks initiated by military forces under the direction of the King of England and to pursue those forces into England and subdue them there, the King of Denmark would be a just conqueror. Given the distinction between unjust and just conquest, any inquiry about whether conquest gives rise to legitimate authority over the conquered realm has to be divided into two questions: (i) Does *unjust* conquest yield legitimate authority?; and (ii) Does *just* conquest yield legitimate authority?

Locke's discussion of the first question is in reality a critique of Hobbes's second account about the appearance of legitimate authority. Hobbes' first account—that of sovereignty by "institution"—involves individuals mutually surrendering all of their rights. Hobbes' second account—that of sovereignty by "acquisition"—involves conquest and submission to the conqueror. Hobbes, of course, holds that *any* conquest is permissible— since nothing is impermissible in the state of nature. Nevertheless, even Hobbes thinks that the vanquished are *not* obligated to obey the conqueror unless they have consented to their subordination to him. Hobbes contends that the vanquished do indeed consent to this subordination; they consent in exchange for the conqueror not exercising his moral liberty to kill them all. Locke rejects this consent argument on the grounds that agreements made under such (undeserved) duress have no binding force. If one allows, as Hobbes does, that the consent of the vanquished is necessary,

> It remains only to be considered, whether *promises extracted by force*, without right, can be thought consent, and *how far they bind*; because whatsoever another gets from me by force, I still retain the right of, and he is obliged presently to restore . . . (1980, II, 186)

When we consider this issue, we must conclude that promises extracted by force cannot obligate.

> [F]or the law of nature laying an obligation on me only by the rules she prescribes, cannot oblige me by the violation of her rules: such is the extorting any thing from me by force. Nor does it at all alter the case to say, *I gave my promise*, no more than it excuses the force, and passes the right, when I put my hand in my pocket, and deliver my purse myself to a thief, who demands it with a pistol at my breast. (1980, II, 186)

Nor, according to Locke, does the fact that the employer of force wears a crown make any difference. For, once again, Locke insists that political kingpins are subject to the same moral norms which apply to all men as men.

> The injury and the crime is equal, whether committed by the wearer of a crown, or some petty villain. The title of the offender, and the number of his followers, make no difference in the offence, unless it be to aggravate it. The only difference is, great robbers punish little ones, to keep them in their obedience, but the great ones are rewarded with laurels and triumphs, because they are too big for the weak hands of justice in this world, and have the power in their own possession, which should punish offenders. (1980, II, 176)

Indeed, Locke's outrage at the capacity of wearers of crowns to get away with actions that are recognized as criminal when performed by ordinary men goes all the way back to *ELN*. There he quotes Cato the Younger's remark that "Thieves committing private theft spend their lives in prison and in chains; public thieves, in gold and in purple" (1997, p.111).

Locke employs a different strategy to argue against the thesis that *just* conquest gives rise to legitimate political authority. The strategy is simply to limit the authority that the just conqueror acquires to authority over the particular individuals who engaged in unjust war against him. Locke accepts without question the standard view of his time that the just conqueror has "an absolute power over the lives of those who by an unjust war have forfeited them" (1980, II, 178). The just victor may put to death or enslave these unjust aggressors. He may parole then on condition of their obedience to him. However, the just conqueror attains this rightful power only over those individuals "who actually assisted, concurred, or consented [presumably *expressly*] to that unjust force that is used against him." The just conqueror acquires legitimate power only over those individuals who "actually abet" the unjust war.

> . . . all the rest are innocent; and he has no more title over the people of that country, who have done him no injury, and so have made no forfeiture of their lives, than he has over any other, who, without any injuries or provocations, have lived upon fair terms with him. (1980, II, 179)

Having no rights over the lives of the innocent, the just conqueror certainly has no title to their estates.

Furthermore, the just conqueror's claim on the estates of those who are guilty of aggression against him or his subjects is very much fenced in. For the liability of the unjust aggressors is limited to the costs which the just conqueror has had to incur "to repair the damages he has sustained by the war, and the defence of his own right" (1980, II, 182). Locke offers a rough calculation of the upper limits of what the unjust vanquished may owe in reparations to the just victors. He concludes that the debt of each landowning abettor of unjust aggression is likely to be no more than two or three years of the harvest from his land. Hence, the value of what is owed in reparations is very much less than the value of the land of the guilty abettors. Therefore, the just conqueror may not in the name of reparations lay claim to the land of the guilty abettors.

Moreover, no matter how extensive the just conqueror's claims to reparations are, they stand second in line behind the claims of the wife and children of the unjust abettor. For prior to and independent of the abettor's unjust actions, his wife and children had rights against him to a share of his estate. That share of his estate is not the abettor's to forfeit. It is not among the assets that are available for making restitution for the damage to others wrought by this abettor's actions. In discussing these claims of the unjust abettor's wife and child, Locke seems to picture the situation as one in which the rights of the wife and children are in conflict with the rights of the just conqueror to reparations. He then asks, "What is to be done in this case?" And, after reciting the fundamental law "that all, as much as may be, should be preserved," he says "if there be not enough to satisfy both . . . , he that hath, and to spare, must remit something of his full satisfaction, to give way to the pressing and preferable title of those who are in danger to perish without it" (1980, II, 183). Thus, Locke seems to be appealing to a utilitarian balancing of rights. Yet, for Locke to put matters in this way is for Locke to miss or misstate the point of his own analysis. The title of the wife and children are "preferable" precisely because those rights antecede the relationship between the abetting husband and the just conqueror. The wife and the children have their rights *and* they are innocent; and, so the just conqueror has no more claim on their share of the estate than he has a claim on the estate of any other innocent.

Finally, Locke points out that the just victor acquires no additional legitimate power "*over those that conquered with him.*" Even if we suppose that William the Conqueror was a just conqueror and through his victory he acquired absolute authority over all the Saxons and Britons, "The *Normans* that came with him, and helped to conquer, and all descended from them, are freemen, and no subjects by conquest . . ." (1980, II, 177). By the close of the seventeenth century any Englishman can plausibly deny that he is a descendent of those conquered Saxons or Britons. Hence, even if William was a just conqueror and just conquest yields absolute power over all the conquered and their descendents, any current Englishman can plausibly deny that William had absolute power over him. In total, then, the *Two Treatises* rebuts four defenses of absolute political authority: the patriarchal theory, the mutual surrender of all rights theory (sovereignty of institution), the submission to conquest theory (sovereignty by acquisition), and the just conquest theory.

Before addressing tyranny and rulers' betrayal of the trust of political society, Locke takes note of the rather special case of the usurper. The usurper is simply an agent who wrongly takes possession of the chief executive office. Such an usurper "has no right to be obeyed" (1980, II, 198); and yet a usurper may exercise the power he has seized with complete propriety. Someone might usurp the office of King of England and then proceed to do nothing except to carry out the duties of that office with extreme care and effectiveness. This is a very different kettle of fish from the individual who acquires the office in a perfectly legitimate way and then proceeds tyrannically to use the power of that office in wrongful and unlawful ways. Here Locke comes close to the nice distinction spelled out in the 1579 treatise, *Vindiciae, Contra Tyrannos* between an officeholder who is "an intruder" and an office-holder who is "an abuser." A reasonable man would much rather be subject to an intruder than an abuser (Lanquet and Morney 1994, p.141).

Tyranny and Dissolution

Tyrants are abusers; tyranny exists when any ruler or assembly of rulers exercises his or its governmental power contrary to right. Locke repeatedly associates rightful action by the magistrate with *lawful* action and wrongful conduct with *willful* conduct. The true king makes "the laws the bounds of his power" while the tyrant "makes all give way to his own will and appetite" (1980, II, 200). The tyrant

> makes not the law, but his will, the rule; and his commands and actions are not directed to the preservation of the properties of the people, but the satisfaction of his own ambition, revenge, covetousness, or any other irregular passion. (1980, II, 199)

Locke's general stance with respect to the authority of a tyrant and the propriety of resistance against tyranny is fairly straightforward.

> . . . whosoever in authority exceeds the power given him by the law, and makes use of the force he has under his command, to compass that upon the subject, which the law allows not, ceases in that to be a magistrate: and acting without authority, may be opposed, as any other man, who by force invades the right of another. (1980, II, 202)

Wrongful action on the part of the magistrate is action contrary to *law*. This requires us to ask what Locke has in mind by "the law" when he talks about uses of force "which the law allows not." It is clear that Locke cannot mean the enacted law. For the enacted law—especially if it is enacted by the tyrannical wrongdoer—may very well allow the actions which Locke says are not allowed by the law. By "the law," Locke has got to mean something like the underlying fundamental law of the land. This was a familiar, albeit difficult, notion within the ideological debates of the seventeenth century (and later). The fundamental law of the land is not statutory law and is not the expression of the will of any individual or group. Yet neither is it simply the law of nature. Rather, it is an accumulated body of legal norms that governs the conduct of all individuals and specifically the conduct of rulers. This body of norms has been partially articulated over time and through various historical contingencies in documents like the Magna Carta and the 1628 Petition of Right, in practices like the monarch's coronation oath, and in salient court decisions. Some of it is yet to be articulated; judges may *discover* more of this law as they apply already recognized principles to new sorts of cases. Moreover, this articulation is reflective of and gives more concrete form to higher principles of natural law. It was this sort of notion of a fundamental legal order which is non-legislated and reflective of basic principles of justice which opponents of Charles I, Charles II, and James II often had in mind when they held that the activities of these monarchs were unlawful.

I have said that this is what Locke has got to mean by "the law" which the tyrant violates. Unfortunately, Locke's appeal to such a notion of law also has got to be tacit at most. For, as we have seen, Locke remains expressly wed to the formula that law requires a conscious and willful lawmaker. This precludes him from seeing law as a grown (non-willed, non-legislated) body of reasonable and just norms for human interaction.[1] Nevertheless, we can best understand Locke's claim that the tyrant violates *the law* by plugging in this notion of the fundamental law of the land. Indeed, Locke's example of an *unlawful* act by an official that may be resisted fits this conjecture quite nicely. His example is the act of a subordinate magistrate who has a legally valid warrant for a man's arrest but who breaks into that man's home to arrest him. According to Locke, this subordinate magistrate "may be opposed as a thief and a robber" (1980, II, 202). But what *law* would this functionary be violating? He would be violating the non-statutory, customary legal norm—reflective no doubt of natural rights to security and property—that each man's home is his castle.

In his chapter "Of Tyranny," Locke focuses on the case of the individual subject who faces a violation of his rights by an officer of the state. Suppose this officer, under pretense of law, comes to seize one's cottage and garden. Locke's view is that, if one can secure the return of one's property by appeal to the public system of law, one will *not* have the right to resist forcibly. For ". . . where the injured party may be relieved, and his damages repaired by appeal to the law, there can be no pretence for force" (1980, II, 205). Suppose, however, the petty officer is acting under orders of the chief magistrate or that the chief magistrate has become so neglectful of his duties that criminal petty officers are not kept in check. Then one is in a state of war vis-a-vis that officer or vis-a-vis the political structure at large and one may lawfully resist the seizure of one's cottage and garden. Against whom may one use harmful or even deadly force? Clearly one may use harmful force against the particular officials who directly threaten one's life, liberty, or estate. No commission or command by the king can immunize his minions against such justified resistance. However, Locke *appears* to hold that "the person of the prince by the law is sacred" and, hence, the king himself is never subject to injurious acts of resistance. If the king himself shows up and seizes your cottage and garden and can be dislodged only by a good beating, you must desist and reconcile yourself to your loss. However, it is difficult to believe that Locke himself accepted the *sacredness* of any prince or the implication of that sacredness, viz., that princes are to be "free from all question or violence, not liable to force, or any judicial censure or condemnation" (1980, II, 205).

Locke also presents a utilitarian-sounding argument for the prince's immunity. This argument calls upon us to compare the harm that will be done by a prince "in his own person" who engages in various scattered injurious acts against his subjects—seizing a cottage here and a lovely young lady there—with the harm that would be done to "the peace of the public, and security of government" if the person of the chief magistrate were not "set out of reach of danger" (1980, II, 205). Only the harm that this "heady prince" does *in his own person* counts because the argument supposes that forcible resistance may be directed at any minions who are doing the prince's dirty work. However, I suspect that Locke does not really accept this argument. I suspect that he is actually mocking complacency about the mischievousness of princes. Here is the statement that Locke provides of why one should not be much concerned about the activities of the heady prince.

> . . . the inconveniency of some particular mischiefs, that may happen sometimes, when a heady prince comes to the throne, are well recompensated by the peace of the public, and security of the government, in the person of the chief magistrate, thus set out of the reach of danger: it being safer for the body, that some few private men should be sometimes in danger to suffer, than that the head of the republic should be easily, and upon slight occasions, exposed. (1980, II, 205)

I ask the reader to imagine *Locke's* reaction to this statement were he to read it in some volume of Filmer or Hobbes. Especially if we remember that this argument is supposed to immunize the prince no matter what type of isolated mischief he is embarked upon, surely Locke's response to this passage would invoke claims from his chapter "Of the State of War."

... I have reason to conclude, that he who would get me into his power without my consent, would use me as he pleased when he got me there, and destroy me too when he had a fancy to it; ... and reason bids me look on him, as an enemy to my preservation, who would take away that freedom which is the fence to it ... (1980, II, 17)

This makes it lawful for a man to *kill a thief*, who has not in the least hurt him, nor declared any design upon his life. ... using force, where he has no right, to get me into his power, let his pretence be what it will, I have no reason to suppose, that he, who would *take away my liberty*, would not, when he had me in his power, take away every thing else. And therefore it is lawful for me to treat him as one who has put himself into a state of war with me, i.e. kill him if I can; for to that hazard does he justly expose himself, whoever introduces a state of war, and is aggressor in it. (1980, II, 18)

The heady prince who justifies immunity for himself on the basis of how crucial that immunity is for "the peace of the public and the security of government" is engaged in the supreme pretense. Contrary to that prince's claim not to be exposed to forcible resistance, Locke himself tells us that *whoever* has initiated a state of war against others "does ... justly expose himself" to being killed.[2] There also seems to be a clue which Locke himself has planted to indicate that he is *not* endorsing the conclusion of the utilitarian argument. Locke says the conclusion of this argument is that "the head of the republic" who is merely engaged in isolated mischief should not be exposed to danger. Yet this cannot mean that any *prince* is immunized from such danger; for, as all of Locke's readers would recognize, no *prince* is the head of any *republic*![3]

In any case, Locke quickly indicates that the alleged special immunity for the prince is only a supposition which he has been entertaining for the sake of argument. Moreover, as we shall see shortly, as soon as the mischief of the prince becomes sufficiently wide-spread that resistance to his activities has a decent chance of success, the mischief-maker loses his status as prince and, hence, any special immunity which might be thought to attach to his "sacred" being. Still, Locke is sensitive to the charge that his doctrine of rightful private resistance may be harmfully disruptive of society. He poses this challenge to himself:

May the *commands* then *of a prince be opposed?* May he be resisted as often as any one shall find himself aggrieved, and but imagine he has not right done him? This will unhinge and overturn all polities, and, instead of government and order, leave nothing but anarchy and confusion. (1980, II, 203)

Isn't this doctrine of rightful resistance merely an invitation to each person to turn to violence whenever he is perturbed by the actions of the prince? Locke's answer is that he is not saying that a man may resist as often as he "*find[s]* himself *aggrieved*" or as often as he "*imagine[s]* he has not right done him." He may resist only when he is correct in his grievance, only when he is correct in his judgment that he has not right done him: ". . . *force* is to be *opposed* to nothing, but to unjust and unlawful *force.*" Any man who turns to force against actions or regimes that he *mistakenly* feels or imagines to be unjust or unlawful "draws on himself a just condemnation both from God and man" (1980, II, 204). Such an individual will not find supporters among his fellow men; hence, he is very likely to be quickly and properly squashed by the just prince. Moreover, if such a man does manage to stir up trouble against a just regime, he is certain eventually to suffer God's wrath. Recognizing these facts, even men who most sincerely take themselves to be aggrieved can see that they should be very cautious about taking up arms. Indeed, even individuals who are in the right and know themselves to be so will have strong prudential reasons not to take up arms as long as they are few and isolated. Speaking of such men, Locke tells us that

. . . though they have a right to defend themselves, and to recover by force what by unlawful force is taken from them; yet the right to do so will not easily engage them in a contest, wherein they are sure to perish . . . (1980, II, 208)

Feasible resistance is possible only when those wielding unlawful power extend their mischief to considerably more people—Locke says "to the majority of the people"—or when those unlawful actions persuade "all" in their consciences "that their law, and with them their estates, liberties, and lives are in danger, and perhaps their religion too"[4] (1980, II, 209). This suggests that, for Locke, justified resistance is feasible when a large number of individuals, each with his own just grievance and each prepared to exercise his own private right of resistance join forces to rid themselves of their common enemy. Yet this is not quite the story which Locke tells.

Political Society as the Agent of Resistance

For, in his final chapter, "Of the Dissolution of Government," the primary actor in widespread justified resistance is that special entity—political society. Political society, not individuals who have been thrown back into a general state of nature, is the bulwark against arbitrary and predatory power. It is political society which, within the bounds of its delegated authority, has established a constitutional structure to secure the lives, liberties, and estates of its members and has authorized particular individuals to act within that structure to secure those rights. Recall, especially, that this structure includes a legislative power which includes the House of Lords, the House of Commons and the monarch and an executive power entrusted to the monarch. Individuals who have agreed to serve in governmental roles have assumed two basic obligations to the members of that political society. The first is to sustain—or at least not to undermine—the constitutional structure which political society has created. The second is to exercise their powers to advance—or at least not to damage—the end for which political society was created, viz., the preservation of the property of those who enter into society.

Consider first the obligation to sustain the constitutional structure. Since Locke thinks of this structure as the creation of political society and thinks of the obligation that individuals in governmental roles have to sustain this structure as an obligation to political society, it is natural for Locke to see political society itself as the aggrieved party when wielders of governmental power undermine or circumvent this structure. Thus, it is political society and individuals as members of political society who stand against attempts to undermine or circumvent the established constitutional order. Political society must be especially wary of the activities of the chief executive. For the chief executive has

... the force, treasure and offices of the state to employ, and [is] often persuading himself, or being flattered by others, that as supreme magistrate he is uncapable of controul.

This chief executive alone

... is in a condition to make great advances toward such changes, under pretence of lawful authority, and has it in his hands to terrify or suppress opposers, as factious, seditious, and enemies to the government. (1980, II, 218)

The chief magistrate undermines the constitutional structure when he "sets up his own arbitrary will in place of the laws, which are the will of the society, declared by the legislative . . ." (1980, II, 214). Imagine, for example, a chief executive who declares that no activities that he orders to be done in the name of national security can be contrary to law even if they are contrary to valid statutes. Similarly, the prince who prevents the legislative from meeting, who unilaterally changes the manner of election to the legislative, or who delivers the people "into the subjection of a foreign power" (1980, II, 217) violates the right of political society to his fulfilling his authorized role within the governmental order.

The second obligation of those who have accepted roles with the governmental structure is to protect—and certainly not to invade—the lives, liberties, and estates of the members of political society. Those charged with legislative or executive responsibilities violate

> . . . *the trust* reposed in them, when they endeavor to invade the property of the subject, and make themselves, or any part of the community, masters, or arbitrary disposers of the lives, liberties, or fortunes of the people. (1980, II, 221)

The offense of those with governmental responsibilities who "take away and destroy the property of the people" (1980, II, 222) has two aspects. First, those agents violate particular rights of life, liberty, or estate. These are the sort of violations of rights that entitle the victim of a heady prince's mischief to resist those mischievous actions—even if it would not be prudent to do so. Second, those agents violate political society's contractual right to their protecting—and certainly their not invading—these rights of subjects. Since this contractual right is a right *acquired by political society* through its agreement with those who have accepted governmental roles, the second aspect of the offense of these officials is an offense against political society.

Locke says that the government is *dissolved* when governmental officials—especially the monarch—violate their first obligation or go beyond isolated and mischievous violations of their second obligation. However, this dissolution of government is not to be confused with a dissolution of political society. Since the actions of wrong-doing officials dissolve the government, such officials no longer have any standing *as officials*. In the case of a wrong-doing king, that individual has "dethroned himself." He has, therefore, put himself back in a state of nature—indeed, in a state of war—with political society. The members of political society may now deal with him "who is no king, as they would any other man, who has put himself in a state of war with them . . ." (1980, II, 239). In addition, since it is the king who has caused the dissolution of government, it is the king who is the rebel, not those who oppose the king. Since the actions of the rebellious king has dissolved the government,

> . . . the people are at liberty to provide for themselves, by erecting a new legislative, differing from the other, by the change of persons, or form, or both, as they shall find it most for their safety and good. (1980, II, 220)

The people need not wait to exercise this liberty until "it is too late, and the evil is past cure" (1980, II, 220). Moreover, Locke is able to dissociate his doctrine of justified resistance from the scary thought that justified resistance involves a return to a general state of nature—even if it would be a Lockean and not a Hobbesian state of nature. Political society, the community, the people, the common-wealth remains in existence throughout the process. A state of nature exists between political society and the dethroned monarch, but not among the individuals who resist that former monarch's unlawful conduct. Finally, the focus on political society as the entity which stands up and asserts *its* rights against the wayward monarch taps into an older antiauthoritarian doctrine of *popular sovereignty*. According to this doctrine, political authority originally resides in the people. Governments and, especially, kings have authority merely as authorized agents of the people. However, Locke's appeal to political society as the aggrieved party and the agent of resistance creates a number of problems.

First, there is the problem of the mysterious nature of this thing called "political society." Second, the associated doctrine of popular sovereignty is not really compatible with the distinctive features of Locke's doctrine. After all, for Locke, there is no *original* political authority; the only original authority is *nonpolitical* individual authority. A limited political authority comes into existence in the form of political society when individuals unify their private rights to act as executors of the law of nature. The authority of the resulting political community or common-wealth is limited because it is created solely for the sake of the more effective and reliable protection of the first-order rights of individuals. In contrast, the doctrine of popular sovereignty takes political authority to be an original right of the people. Political society's creation of a legislative is an exercise of *its* "native and original right" to preserve itself (1980, II, 220). Since the people's political authority does not arise from authorization from individuals, the people's authority is not limited by rights retained by those individuals. Thus, the doctrine of popular sovereignty can easily be employed on behalf of populist authoritarian conclusions. Third, Locke's appeal to the doctrine of popular sovereignty makes the *will* of the people—in contrast to the *law*—the ultimate measure of the legitimacy of governmental action. In the chapter, "Of Tyranny," the focus is on the individual victim of the mischievous prince; and there Locke tells us that it is the *law* which stands against the arbitrary and willful power of the monarch. In contrast, in the final chapter, "Of the Dissolution of Government," the focus shifts to the people as the aggrieved party; and there Locke says that it is the *will* of the people, "the public will," which stands against the arbitrary and willful monarch. Instead of our having a contrast between law (which is a manifestation of reason) and will, we get a contrast between two wills—the will which is "the *essence and union of society*" (1980, II, 212) and the will of the monarch.

Fourth, there is a serious discrepancy between what Locke tells us about the membership of political society when he presents his doctrine of consent and what Locke needs to presume about the membership in political society when he discusses political society's resistance against a wrongdoing monarch. The doctrine of consent allows us to count as members of a political society all inheritors (and purchasers) of land which is tied to that society plus all who have expressly declared their membership. This leaves many individuals as nonmembers. That is why Locke invokes tacit consent to make these remaining individuals subject to the law. Whether that appeal to tacit consent works or not, all those individuals remain non-members of the fairly exclusive club which is political society. Hence, if being a just resister requires that one be a member of political society, just resisters are going to be far more scarce than Locke presumes them to be. It looks like the way around this problem would be to hold that individuals defending their rights *as individuals*, rather than *as members of political society*, are the just resisters.

Fifth, recall Locke's insistence that the decisions and actions of political society must be governed by majority vote (1980, II, 96–99). It follows that no member's resistance to James II or support for the intervention of William of Orange could have been justified unless a majority of the members of political society—whoever they are—had voted for this resistance or support. Yet no such vote took place; and it does not seem

ever to occur to Locke that such a vote within political society was necessary for the revolution to be glorious.

All of these problems could have been avoided if Locke had simply
invoked the rights of individuals *as individuals* (to the nonviolation of
their rights *and* to the structure of governance that they have individually
authorized). Locke's account of the "original" of government authority
would have been philosophically more streamlined had he cut out the
middleman—political society. He might, instead, have envisioned individuals in a state of nature directly contracting with a government for the
provision of known law, indifferent judges, and the enforcement of
known law and judicial decisions just as individuals may directly contract
with a manor cleaning service for the upkeep of their manors. Included
in the individual's contract with the government would be the individual's transfer to the government of his state of nature right to be an
executor of the law of nature and his agreement to pay for the government's provision of law, judicial services, and enforcement.[5] Presumably,
individuals who recognize the need for divided authority within government will only contract with a government which embodies that division
of authority.

Indeed, if we review the core elements of Locke's account of wide-
spread justified resistance, we can see that they need not be tied to the
troubling concept of political society. The first of those core elements is
simply each individual's liberty to stand in defense of his rights—both to
his life, liberty, and estate and to the form of governance which he has
authorized. This individual liberty comes out most clearly in Locke's
response to the proposal that individuals should submit to violations of
rights for the sake of peace.

> If the innocent honest man must quietly quit all he has, for peace sake,
> to him who will lay violent hands upon it, I desire it may be considered,
> what a kind of peace there will be in the world, which consists only of
> violence and rapine; and which is to be maintained only for the benefit
> of robbers and oppressors. Who would not think it an admirable peace
> betwix the mighty and the mean, when the lamb, without resistance,
> yielded his throat to be torn by the imperious wolf? (1980, II, 228)

The next core element is the caution which individuals will exercise in
determining whether they will stand in defense of their rights and join
forces against existing political regimes. Locke maintains that men will

be slow—perhaps slower than they ought to be—to risk their lives and fortunes in resistance:

> . . . *revolutions happen* not upon every little mismanagement in public affairs. *Great mistakes* in the ruling part, many wrong and inconvenient laws, and all the slips of human frailty, will be born by the people without mutiny or murmur. (1980, II, 225)

Individuals will converge upon resistance only

> . . . if a long train of abuses, prevarications, and artifices, all tending the same way, make the design visible to the people, and they cannot but feel what they lie under, and see whither they are going . . . (1980, II, 225)

Only when the mischief has "grown general, and the ill designs of the rulers become visible" (1980, II, 230) will the people stir to resistance.

The final core element is Locke's answer to the recurring question, "Who shall be judge?" Locke's immediate answer is "*The people shall be judge*" (1980, II, 240). And he does go on to speak of the "the body of the people" (1980, II, 241) being the proper umpire when there is a dispute about whether the prince or the legislative have acted contrary to their trust. This fits with Locke's view that it is political society which has extended that trust to the prince or the legislative assembly and that the state of nature which exists when that trust is broken only obtains between political society and the trust-breaker. Nevertheless, the judgments that Locke envisions are private judgments by discrete individuals, not judgments by some collective, unified entity. The soundness of any individual's judgment does not at all depend on its being part of the majority's judgment. Of course, God in heaven is the only infallible judge; yet no human being can elude the responsibility of judging for himself.

> . . . *every man* is *judge* for himself, as in all other cases, so in this, whether another hath put himself into a state of war with him, and whether he should appeal to the Supreme Judge, as Jeptha did.[6] (1980, II, 241)

In the absence of a common judge on earth, "the injured party must judge for himself, when he will think fit to make use of that appeal, and put himself upon it" (1980, II, 242). To appeal to heaven, of course, is not to appeal for God's intervention. Rather it is to take up the sword on the basis of one's own judgment that one's cause is just and one's *hope* that one is correct. The most telling phrase in the passage about the appeal to the Supreme Judge is "as in all other cases." Ultimately, each man has nothing to go on except his own judgment. This is the fundamental lesson that Locke draws from his epistemological investigations. There is no body of knowledge provided to us by the innate constitution of our minds or by tradition; we can only proceed by way of sense perception and reason—which necessarily is one's own sense perception and reason.

Inescapable Private Judgment

Recall though that we are supposed to overcome the inconveniences of the state of nature by resigning up our private judgment about how the law of nature is to be articulated and enforced. Does the fact that private judgment is inescapable mean that the state of nature is inescapable? We can identify two ways through which the inconveniences of the state of nature can be avoided even though private judgment is inescapable. The first way involves *replacing* the private judgments that generate those inconveniences with *other* private judgments that are less apt to generate conflict and tumult. We have seen that, especially as economic and social life becomes more specialized and complex, the law of nature does not provide determinate answers to questions about where the boundaries of persons' rights lie and what the proper reparation or punishment for a given violation of rights is. This indeterminacy allows there to be disagreement among reasonable men in the state of nature about where the boundaries lie and what the proper reparation or punishment for a given boundary crossing is. To avoid the conflict which comes from there being this range of reasonable judgments, rational individuals in the state of nature agree to abide by whatever *reasonable* judgment is reached by their jointly established authority. They agree, in short, to base their decisions about compliance not on their private judgment about whether the public pronouncement is correct but, rather, on their (inescapably) private judgment about whether it is reasonable. It is only when the decision of the established political order falls outside of the range of the reasonable—it is only when it is not reasonable to construe the decision as falling within the range of the reasonable—that the individual has grounds for avoidance or resistance. In *A Letter Concerning Toleration,* Locke says that

. . . the private judgment of any Person concerning a Law enacted in Political Matters, for the publick Good, does not take away the Obligation of that Law, nor deserve a Dispensation. But if the Law indeed be concerning things that lie not within the Verge of the Magistrate's Authority . . . men are not in these cases obliged by that Law, against their Consciences . . . (1983, p.48)

What Locke especially has in mind as law that does not lie within the verge of the magistrate's authority is law mandating religious belief or practice. However, Locke goes on to address the situation in which the magistrate believes that the promulgation of some law is within his authority to act for the public good while his subjects believe it is not within his authority because it is neither "in the Constitution of the Government granted him, nor ever was in the power of the People to grant" (1983, p.49). As one would expect, at this point Locke says that the subjects must act on their private judgments, that is, they must appeal to heaven. The crucial point, though, is that each subject's private judgment is a judgment about whether or not the magistrate's action falls within the verge of his authority. The subject remains under an obligation to abide by the magistrate's decree as long as it can reasonably be viewed as being in accord with his authority to serve the ends for which government has been created. In parallel fashion, there can be reasonable dispute about what is the best way for governmental officials to conform to or support the established constitutional order. To avoid conflict among good-willed individuals on the basis of this indeterminacy, their contract with those officials can only forbid those officials from engaging in actions which cannot reasonably be construed as conforming to the constitutional order. Individuals still must make private judgments; but those judgments about whether the officials have stepped beyond the range of their reasonable choices. Since the range of reasonable choices is greater than the range of correct choices, private judgments by individuals about whether some action or policy falls within the former range is less likely to generate conflict than private judgments about whether some action or policy falls within the latter range.

The second way the inconveniences of the state of nature can be avoided even though private judgment is inescapable is that it is more costly to the individual to disregard or resist governmental judgments than the judgments of other state of nature individuals. This greater cost will make individuals less prone to resist government decisions which they take to be incorrect or which they take to be unreasonable than they would be to resist like judgments by individuals in the state of nature. In practice, then, a reasonable individual will not resist the decisions of governmental officials until it is clear that those decisions are unreasonable exercises of power which are likely to impose significant damage on him. This is why resistance is justified and likely to occur only when "*a long train of actions shew the councils* all tending that way." At that point, "how can a man any more hinder himself from being persuaded in his own mind, which way things are going; or from casting about how to save himself . . . ?" (1980, II, 210) At that point, also, others will see the justice of one's resistance or see the danger to themselves in the "way things are going." Hence, the actual alternative to "the boundless will of tyranny" is not resistance whenever anyone feels aggrieved but, rather

. . . that rulers should be sometimes liable to be opposed, when they grow exorbitant in the use of their power, and employ it for the destruction, and not the preservation of the properties of their people . . . (1980, II, 229)

6

Locke on Toleration

Locke's *A Letter Concerning Toleration,* was published in the same heady year as the *Two Treatises of Government* and *An Essay Concerning Human Understanding.* Composed while Locke was in exile in Holland, *A Letter* is the centerpiece of Locke's fairly radical defense of religious toleration. The issue of religious toleration and the magistrate's authority (or lack of authority) to prescribe religious beliefs or practices animated Locke throughout his intellectual life. His very early essays, the "Two Tracts on Government," upheld the magistrate's right and obligation to mold religious belief and practice within his realm. Locke's first clearly anti-authoritarian work, the remarkable 1667 "An Essay on Toleration," is a robust defense of religious liberty. While Locke was composing the *Two Treatises* in the late 1670s and early 1680s, he was at work with his friend James Tyrrell on another defense of toleration.[1] In support of the claims of *A Letter,* Locke composed a lengthy second and a massive third letter on toleration (1690 and 1692) and he was still at work on a fourth letter when he died.[2]

A Letter is not a marvel of organizational clarity. Although it is full of good arguments and powerful denunciations of religious persecution, it utterly lacks the orderly argumentative development of the *Second Treatise.* One of my goals in this chapter is to delineate an overall structure for Locke's defense of toleration within which his various particular arguments have more or less determinate places. I begin this chapter by representing Locke's doctrine of toleration as a straightforward application of the rights-based, individualist liberalism of the *Second Treatise.* This has the side benefit of highlighting the extent to which Locke reaffirms—in the case of "An Essay on Toleration" anticipates—the doctrine of the *Second Treatise* within his writings on religious liberty. I will then present *A Letter* as an investigation of whether the framework of the Lockean state really does exclude the magistrate's use of coercion to suppress religious beliefs or practices or whether that restrictive framework ought to be loosened so as to allow the magistrate's employment of such coercion. Other arguments by Locke are cast as responses to anticipated criticisms of his developing doctrine.

A very salient refrain throughout Locke's letters concerning toleration is his claim that every religion is orthodox to itself. We shall have to consider what Locke means by this claim, how it is related to the inescapability of private judgment, and how this claim is supposed to support the case for toleration. Finally, Locke's brief for toleration was strongly and ably opposed by Jonas Proast, a chaplain at All Souls College, Oxford. Locke's second letter was a response to Proast's 1690 critique of *A Letter*. Locke's third letter was a response to Proast's 1691 critique of Locke's second letter. And Locke's unfinished fourth letter was intended as a response to Proast's 1704 critique of Locke's third letter (Proast, 1984). There are many twists and turns in this almost interminable dispute. I will attend directly to only one feature of it, viz., Proast's counterproposal that the magistrate may use force only to insure that people pay attention to the case for true religion.[3] As we proceed through the details of Locke's position on religious liberty, we should remain alert to the ways in which Locke's arguments, however embedded they are in the controversies of his day, constitute a template for the general defense of the liberty of individuals to pursue their own conceptions of the good in their own chosen ways—even when those conceptions and chosen ways are damned by others.

The Lockean State and Religious Liberty

Near the beginning of "An Essay on Toleration," Locke nicely anticipates his later account of the rise of political authority devoted to the protection of men's rights:

> . . .the whole trust, power, and authority of the magistrate is vested in him for no other purpose but to be made use of for the good, preservation, and peace of men in that society over which he is set, and therefore . . . this alone is and ought to be the standard and measure according to which he ought to square and proportion his law, and model and frame his government. . . . [M]agistrates and polities . . . are only made to preserve men in this world from the fraud and violence

of one another; so that what was the end of erecting government ought alone to be the measure of its proceeding. (1997, p.135)

Near the outset of *A Letter*, Locke reminds us that

It is the Duty of the Civil Magistrate, by the impartial Execution of equal Laws, to secure unto all the People in general, and to every one of his Subjects in particular, the just Possession of the things belonging to this Life. . . . the Magistrate [is] armed with the Force and Strength of all his Subjects, in order to the punishment of those that violate any other Man's Rights. (1983, p.26)

And about two thirds of the way through *The Letter*, Locke returns to his basic doctrine about why magistrates and polities are needed.

But the pravity of Mankind being such, that they have rather injuriously prey upon the Fruits of other mens Labours, than take pains to provide for themselves; the necessity of preserving Men in the possession of what honest industry has already acquired, and also of preserving their Liberty and strength, whereby they may acquire what they further want; obliges Men to enter into Society with one another; that by mutual Assistance, and joint Force, they may secure unto each other their Proprieties in the things that contribute to the Comfort and Happiness of this Life . . . (1983, p.47)

Locke's emphasis here on men's disposition to prey upon the fruits of other men's labors resonates with his claim throughout *A Letter* that religious persecutors are in reality much more interested in seizing the property of those they persecute than in saving their souls. We must remember "how easily the pretence of Religion, and the care of Souls, serves for a Cloak to Covetousness, Rapine, and Ambition" (1983, p.43).[4]

Since the role of the magistrate is limited to protecting men from invasions of their property and since others' religious activities are not invasive of men's property, the magistrate's authority does not extend to interference in others' religious activities. When the Catholic believes that the Bread is the Body of Christ, "he does no injury thereby to his neighbor." When the Jew does not believe in the New Testament, "he does not thereby alter any thing in mens Civil Rights" (1983, p.46).

Moreover, forcible interference with others' religious activities will itself be invasive of their rights. Hence the magistrate is bound to protect individuals against such interference. "[P]rotection from such injury is one of the ends of a commonwealth, and so every man has a right to toleration" (1823, p.212). As we noted at the close of the previous chapter, the Lockean conception of the limits on the magistrate's authority implies that religion is beyond "the Verge of the Magistrate's Authority" (1983, p.48). That is to say, all religious activities in which individuals are merely exercising their freedom to dispose of their lives, liberties, and properties as they see fit are beyond the range of the magistrate's authority. This is not because they are performed out of religious conviction or for a religious purpose, but simply because they are exercises by individuals of their freedom to dispose as they see fit of what is theirs. Indeed, at this fundamental level, there is no *special* case for religious liberty. That one's action is done out of religious conviction or for a religious purpose neither adds to nor subtracts from one's right to engage in that action. If it is within my rights to consume wine and bread for gastronomical purposes, it is also within my rights to consume them for religious purposes. If it is not within my rights to sacrifice infants for gastronomical purposes, it is also not within my rights to sacrifice them for religious purposes. Whether I have the right to consume the wine depends quite simply on whether the wine is mine. Whether I have a right to sacrifice the infant depends upon whether the infant is my property (which it is not, even if it is my child).[5]

Locke asks whether the magistrate must allow someone who wishes to sacrifice a calf to do so. For though that person may think it well-pleasing to God that the calf be sacrificed, others may well think that it will offend God. Locke's answer is that the permissibility of the sacrifice depends upon who *owns* the calf. If that person is the owner, then he must be allowed to sacrifice the calf whereas, of course, if another is the owner, it is the magistrate's duty to prevent the killing of the animal.[6] We understand how *all* persons can enjoy religious liberty only when we understand that religious liberty consists in each individual enjoying the freedom of disposing *of himself and his possessions* as he sees fit in matters of religious conviction and practice. Just as perfect liberty in general depends upon mine and thine, so too does perfect religious liberty. The fact that the basis for Tom's liberty to sacrifice the calf is his ownership of that calf and not the righteousness of the sacrifice or the sacrifice being well-pleasing to God has a vital implication. It is that others can affirm and respect Tom's liberty without at all endorsing the sacrifice as righteous or well-pleasing to God. Hence, others can affirm and respect Tom's liberty without expecting that their tolerance of Tom's unrighteous conduct will bring God's wrath down *upon them*.

Still, we may need to ask whether political authority really is as limited as Locke's general political doctrine takes it to be. After all, one might argue, the *Second Treatise* pretty much presumes that men are only concerned about earthly matters, about how they can best arrange for comfortable self-preservation. The great end of men, viz., the salvation of their souls, is almost completely simply ignored or set aside in the argument that runs through the *Second Treatise*. However, if for each individual the salvation of his soul—or, in more secular terms, the living of an upright and noble life—is truly the most important end, might not rational individuals with this end in mind seek to establish a political regime with the authority to assist themselves or others in their quest for salvation (or uprightness or nobility)?

Locke begins his response to the possibility that men might entrust their salvation to the magistrate by denying that any rational man can *unconditionally* authorize *any* other person—prince or subject—*to judge for him* what is the way to salvation.

> . . . no man can so far abandon the care of his own Salvation, as *blindly* to leave it to the choice of another, whether Prince or Subject, to prescribe to him what Faith or Worship he shall embrace. For no Man can, if he would, conform his Faith to the Dictates of another. (1983, p.26, emphasis added)

As a rational being with judgmental powers, one cannot leave off judging the judgments of the church that one has joined. This is why, according to Locke, churches are voluntary societies not only in the sense that one's membership must be chosen but also in the sense that every member retains the right to withdraw.

To authorize the magistrate *as magistrate* to advance the salvation of souls would be to authorize the magistrate's use or threat of force to advance that end. This, according to Locke, no rational individual would do because neither force nor the threat of force can advance the salvation of souls. The reason for this is that salvation is obtained only through "the inward and full perswasion of the mind" (1983, p.26) and this inward persuasion cannot be produced by "outward force."

"Confiscation of Estate, Imprisonment, Torments, nothing of that nature can have any such Efficacy as to make Men change the inward Judgment that they have framed of things" (1983, p.27). This is a central premise in Locke's argument against the magistrate having the authority to use or threaten force in religious matters. It is far from clear that this premise is correct. But I shall contend that Locke has an adequate substitute for it.

Locke correctly believes that the magistrate will not be able to convert a non-Christian subject to genuine belief in the divinity of Christ simply by depriving the subject of this or that portion of his property or by cutting off one or another of his fingers or by threatening the subject with such treatment. The threats of such treatment may make the subject *want* to believe—or *seem* to believe—what the magistrate wants him to believe. But, at least at any given moment, the subject's desire to believe in, for example, the divinity of Christ, will not generate that belief in the subject. For, ". . . to believe this or that to be true, does not depend upon our Will" (1983, p.46). Nevertheless, may not the use or threat of force *over time* generate the intended belief? If, for a long enough time, the subject is made to want to believe in the divinity of Christ, might this not bring the subject to genuine inward belief? It seems that either through making people strongly enough *want* to believe for a long enough period of time or through otherwise drilling beliefs into them, people can be *made* to have certain inward persuasions. Brainwashing does sometimes work. So Locke seems mistaken in his belief that coercion can never produce inward belief. Of course, from the fact that the magistrate could sometimes coerce people into having the right inward convictions, it does not follow that rational individuals would authorize the magistrate to employ coercion whenever he judges it to be apt. Indeed, in his responses to Proast, Locke puts a good deal of emphasis on the distinction between showing that coercion might "accidentally" yield some desirable end and showing that it characteristically and reliably yields that end. He argues that rational individuals would not authorize the magistrate to coerce for religious purposes on the meager grounds that such coercion will sometimes have the desired effect (1823, pp.69–70).

Still, Locke really would like to have a credible premise that supports the conclusion that coercion *cannot* serve the purpose of salvation. We have seen that the premise that coercion cannot produce inward persuasion is not so credible. Consider instead the premise that coercion cannot produce *freely adopted* belief. This seems to be necessarily true; if a belief is the product of coercion, it is not freely adopted. Moreover, this premise seems to serve Locke's purpose nicely because it is plausible that religious belief must have the feature of being freely adopted if it is really to be pleasing to God, that is, if it is really to be salvific. Only a fervent belief that is freely adopted will be to the credit of the believer. Since the magistrate's coercion cannot produce freely adopted belief in his subjects, Locke can draw the conclusion that the magistrate's use of coercion cannot advance the salvation of his subjects; hence, they have no reason to authorize that use of coercion.

Locke offers a further reason for why rational individuals would not authorize the magistrate's use or threat of force for religious purposes. Here, for the sake of argument we are to assume that magistrates can through coercion "convince and change Mens minds." Even given this assumption, authorization for the magistrate's coercion will only be sensible if the magistrate will induce *true* beliefs in his subjects. However, according to Locke, it is quite unlikely that the magistrate will have hit upon the "one Truth," the "one way to Heaven" (1983, p.27). More precisely, each subject has a better chance of hitting upon the "one Truth" if the magistrate is barred from imposing his religious beliefs than the magistrate has of hitting on the "one Truth" if he has the power to impose his religious beliefs. Each subject has a better chance relying upon his own judgment in a situation in which religious beliefs can be freely expressed and debated than he has being subjected to the magistrate's judgment in a situation in which the magistrate does not allow religious beliefs to be freely expressed and debated. One consideration in support of this contention is simply that the magistrate "certainly is less concerned for my Salvation than I my self am" (1983, p.37). The more interesting consideration offered by Locke is his optimistic thesis that people are most likely to arrive at truths if political constraints on the professing of speculative opinions are removed. "For Truth certainly would do well enough, if she were once left to shift for her self." For Locke true belief will have vitality and strength only if truth "makes her way into the Understanding by her own Light" rather than through "any borrowed force Violence can add to her" (1983, p.46). However, Locke never really works out the probabilistic comparison I have formulated above; and one suspects that something other than this comparison is really driving his opposition to handing control over one's religious beliefs to the magistrate. I believe that this something else is precisely his sense that, even if the magistrate would make one believe the "one Truth," this induced belief would not assist one's salvation. For this inward conviction would, by hypothesis, not be freely adopted. Subjects who authorize such a use of coercion will have "quit the light of their own Reason, and oppose[d] the Dictates of their own Consciences, and blindly . . . resign[ed] themselves to the Will of their Governors . . ." (1983, p.27).

Further Considerations against the Magistrate's Authority in Religious Matters

Thus, no rational individual in the state of nature would authorize the magistrate to use or threaten force *against himself* in order to promote his salvation. But might rational individuals in the state of nature authorize the magistrate to use or threaten force *against others* who are engaged in self-damning activity—assuming that such activity can be identified? There are three possible bases for such an authorization: (i) the right to self-defense; (ii) the right to engage in paternalist interventions to forcibly prevent others from harming themselves; and (iii) the right to suppress immoral conduct in others even if it is not rights-violating conduct. If the first basis is sound, then even within the restrictive framework of the Lockean state, the magistrate may move coercively against self-damning agents. If the second or third basis is sound, then the magistrate has authority to use coercion against self-damning agents because that restrictive framework has been loosened. Locke, however, denies the soundness of each of these proposed bases for authorizing the magistrate to act against the individual who is heading toward damnation.

Let us continue to suppose that the magistrate can identify those whose religious beliefs or practices have put them on a path to perdition. How might more orthodox individuals construe the magistrate's suppression of these self-damning beliefs or actions as an exercise of their right of self-defense? Two possible rationales come to mind. First, the more orthodox might think that God will condemn them simply for tolerating such beliefs or practices. They may think that God takes them to be obligated through their agent, the magistrate, to cleanse the world of damnable religious beliefs or practices. The magistrate, acting on behalf of his innocent subjects, protects them from God's wrath by persecuting the religious deviants in their midst. Second, the more orthodox might think that they are in danger of being infected by these hellish beliefs or practices. The only or best way to contain the infection is to quarantine or eradicate it. Just as the magistrate may, under his authority to protect the rights of his subjects, tear down a house through which the contagion of a fire will spread to other houses, so too may the magistrate tear down a church or a preacher through whom the contagion of damning beliefs will spread to his innocent subjects.

Locke rejects both of these self-defense rationales. Here his key premise is that each individual is responsible for his own salvation. All human salvation is abstractly speaking good, but each individual is directly rationally concerned with his own salvation. After all, for each individual his ultimate happiness lies in his own salvation. So, if each rationally seeks his own happiness, each rationally seeks his own salvation.[7] "The care, therefore, of every man's Soul belongs unto himself, and is to be left unto himself" (1983, p.35). Each individual's responsibility for his own salvation would be radically compromised if each individual's salvation was hostage to others' attaining their salvation. For, then, each would be unable to secure one's own salvation without also securing others' salvation. And if others view their salvation as being held hostage to mine, they will be moved to prevent me from taking responsibility for my own salvation whenever they disagree with me about what promotes a soul's salvation. Hence, each individual's being responsible for his own salvation requires that each *let* others go their own way—either to salvation or damnation. Hence, God will not punish one for letting others travel on the road to perdition:

> If any man err from the right way, it is his own misfortune, no injury to thee: Nor therefore art thou to punish him in the things of this Life, because thou supposest he will be miserable in that which is to come. (1983, p.31)

Thus, there is no basis for the magistrate to force others on to the right way so as to protect the subjects who are themselves on the right path from God's anger at them for allowing others to err.

What about the proposed infection rationale? Locke sometimes seems to say that others going down the path to damnation cannot possibly prejudice one's own salvation. "Every man . . . has the supreme and absolute authority of judging for himself. And the Reason is, because no body else is concerned in it, *nor can receive any prejudice* from his Conduct therein" (1983, p.47, emphasis added). This last claim seems true only under certain narrow conditions. Others traveling down that road to perdition cannot prejudice me if I know or firmly believe that theirs is a road to perdition or if they in no way exhort or tempt me to journey with them. Now we have been assuming that the magistrate and his more orthodox subjects know or firmly believe that the religious deviants are on the wrong path. For the rationale for the use of coercion that is under consideration is that coercion is to be used to protect the currently *right-minded* subjects from infection. But suppose that I do not know or firmly believe that the deviants' road leads to damnation and they seek to persuade me to join them. Surely their attempts to persuade me *might* lead me from a true to a false path and, hence, be greatly prejudicial to me. Perhaps that is what has already happened to these poor deviants. Does this constitute a rationale for the magistrate stepping in to defend me by at least silencing religious deviants?

Locke has to answer negatively on the grounds that the situation now is one in which there are competing views about what the right path is and each person's best bet for arriving at the right path is to attend to the exhortations of all the contending parties. What is crucial here is Locke's thought that there is a greater tendency for truth to be detected when there is unrestricted public competition among ideas than when the magistrate is charged with identifying and enforcing the truth. Locke must acknowledge that there is a risk of being persuaded to exchange a salvific view for a damning view; but that risk is more than counterbalanced by the opportunity to be moved from a damning view to a salvific one. So, simply in terms of eternal payoff, it is rational to wager against a system in which the magistrate seeks to identify and enforce the truth. In addition, that system imposes on individuals the worldly costs of being subjected to the magistrate's coercion (1823, p.76). Locke offers a further argument for why the risk from others' attempts to convert one to beliefs or practices that may be paths to perdition does not justify the *forcible* suppression of those beliefs or practices. It is that force is not necessary to resist conversion. For ". . . no man or society of men can, by their opinions in religion or ways of worship, do any man who differed from them any injury, which he could not avoid or redress if he desired it, *without the help of force*" (1823, p.212, emphasis added).

We turn now to the suggestion that the magistrate's use or threat of force in religious matters might have a paternalist rationale. Once again, of course, Locke can invoke his argument that the magistrate is unlikely to know better than the individual operating within a religiously tolerant society which paths are damning and his argument that the magistrate's coercion cannot produce freely adopted belief. What is striking, however, is that Locke insists that even if the magistrate were to know which beliefs were damning and which were salvific and could coerce individuals to adopt the salvific beliefs, he still would not be justified in using that coercion. This is because of Locke's steadfast anti-paternalism. Nothing could be more obvious to Locke than that coercive paternalist interventions in persons' worldly endeavors is preposterously and unacceptably meddlesome:

> No man complains of the ill management of his Neighbour's Affairs. No man is angry with another for an Error committed in sowing his Land, or in marrying his Daughter. No body corrects a Spendthrift for consuming his Substance in Taverns. Let any man pull down, or build, or make whatsoever Expences he pleases, no body murmurs, no body controuls him; he has his Liberty. (1983, p.34)

Locke notes, however, that this willingness to let people make their own mistakes does not in fact carry over to religious error:

> ... if any man do not frequent the Church, if he do not there conform his Behavior exactly to the accustomed Ceremonies, or if he brings not his Children to be initiated in the Sacred Mysteries of this or the other Congregation; this immediately causes an Uproar. The Neighbourhood is filled with Noise and Clamour. Every one is ready to be the Avenger of so great a Crime. (1983, p.34)

Yet, if individuals should be allowed to go about their nonreligious business in their own chosen and possibly foolish ways, they should also be allowed to go about their religious business in their own possibly foolish ways. What matters in both cases is that they are minding their own business. Locke may also be suggesting that the difference in reaction is so striking that some special explanation needs to be given for the uproar that attends religious deviation. The special explanation he offers is that some people have learned how to use a pretense of "Love for the Truth" as a device for "prey[ing] upon the Fruits of other mens Labours" (1983, p.47) or for satisfying their desire for "Temporal Dominion" (1983, p.35). For if the responder's concern really were for the welfare of the deviating party, he would hardly respond as religious persecutors do:

> ... it will be very difficult to persuade men of Sense, that he, who with dry Eyes, and satisfaction of mind, can deliver his Brother unto the

Executioner, to be burnt alive, does sincerely and heartily concern himself to save that Brother from the Flames of Hell in the World to come. (1983, p.35)

Still, the central point is Locke's radical anti-paternalism. After he asserts that "The care . . . of every man's Soul belongs unto himself . . . ," he immediately poses the question, "But what if he neglect the Care of his Soul?" His response is that a man's neglect of his soul no more authorizes others to interfere coercively than his neglect of his health or his estate:

> Laws provide, as much as possible, that the Goods and Health of Subjects be not injured by the Fraud or Violence of others; they do not guard them from the Negligence or Ill-husbandry of the Possessors themselves. No man can be forced to be Rich or Healthful, whether he will or no. Nay, God himself will not save men against their wills. (1983, p.35)

God himself, who certainly knows what beliefs are crucial to salvation and who, if anyone, can cause those beliefs to be appropriately inward and autonomous, will not interfere with an individual's own choice to head down a highly erroneous path.

Locke continues to express this strong anti-paternalism in *A Second Letter Concerning Toleration* where he maintains that even if the magistrate's forcible interference is useful and necessary for some desirable end, it does not follow that the interference is permissible. For two conditions are requisite before an action which ordinarily would be wrongful can be permissible. One condition is that the act "be directly useful for the procuring some greater good." The other condition is that "he who does it has commission and power [i.e., right] so to do" (1823, pp.112–13). One of Locke's examples is a man who has a stone that "the most skilful surgeon in the world" can remove. Although the act of cutting the man would be useful and necessary, it does not follow that "there is a right somewhere to cut him, whether he will or no." There can be "no commission, no right, without the patient's own consent" (1823, p.113).[8] Locke's other example is of "nations in the West Indies" in which people have authorized their prince to lead them in warfare against their common enemies but have not authorized the prince to be the executor of the law of nature within their society. Even though the prince's acting in this way would be beneficial, "it falls not within the compass of those princes' jurisdiction to punish any one of the society for injuring another" (1823, p.121). In the absence of actual consent, the prince has no commission, no right, to engage in this punishment even if it is useful and necessary.

Locke also considers whether there is a moralistic rationale for the magistrate stepping in and forcibly suppressing immoral—albeit, not rights-violating—religious beliefs or practices. Isn't idolatry a sin? And should not the role of the magistrate extend to the punishment of sin? Locke answers the second question in the negative. It does not follow from some action being sinful that it ought to be punished by the magistrate. Indeed, Locke provides us with a significant list of sins the punishment of which is outside the jurisdiction of the magistrate:

> . . . it does not belong unto the Magistrate to make use of his Sword in punishing everything, indifferently, that he takes to be a sin against God. Covetousness, Uncharitableness, Idleness, and many other things are sins, by the consent of all men, which yet no man ever said were to be punished by the Magistrate. The reason is, because they are not prejudicial to other mens Rights, nor do they break the publick Peace of Societies. (1983, pp.43–4)

The limitation of the role of the magistrate to the suppression of acts of violence and fraud is not to be transgressed for either paternalist or moralist purposes.

There is one further argument for state action against religious dissidents that might be classified as a self-defense argument. Whenever religious dissidents gather, they grumble and begin to plan seditious activities. Hence, in order to maintain the public peace, a heavier hand should be employed against these dissidents. Locke's nice response to this is to ask, *why* do those who are denied equal religious liberty complain when they are among their own and *why* are they ill-willed toward the government? *Why* do those who are not permitted to meet in public tend much more than others to meet in secret? The answers, of course, are that these individuals meet in secret because they are not allowed to meet publically; and they chaff under the hand of government because it is already a heavy and unjust hand. The solution is not more oppression but rather liberty:

> . . . let those Dissenters enjoy but the same Privileges in Civils as his other Subjects, and he will quickly find that these Religious Meetings

will be no longer dangerous . . . Oppression raises Ferments, and makes men struggle to cast off an uneasie and tyrannical Yoke. (1983, p.52)

If, instead of persecuting anabaptists, the magistrate denied equal freedom to people with gray eyes, soon gray eyed people would be meeting in secret to plan resistance against the magistrate. Whose action then would be "the very Root of all the Mischief?" (1983, p.53) Desirable religious order arises from liberty, not oppression.

There are, however, some limits on the toleration that Locke recommends. Given the association of Catholicism with the authoritarian impulses of Charles II and James II and with the brutal regimes of Spain, Portugal, and France, it is not surprising that toleration is to be withheld from Catholics on essentially political rather than religious doctrinal grounds. Churches like the Church of Rome are not to be tolerated if they refuse to preach and practice toleration or if they assign "any peculiar Privilege of Power above other Mortals, in Civil Concernments" (1983, p.50) to members of their own Church. Nor is any Church to be tolerated if membership in it amounts to placing oneself under "the Protection and Service of another Prince" (1983, p.50), that is, the Pope. Finally, no Church is to be tolerated which teaches—as Catholicism was thought to teach—that promises to "heretics," that is, Protestants, may be broken at will. This last and still essentially political consideration also rules out toleration for atheists. For, according to Locke, those who deny the existence of God and, therefore, deny the existence of eternal punishment and reward will not take themselves to be bound by their word. Here Locke's divine voluntarist doctrine reasserts itself.

Locke versus Proast

A persistent refrain throughout Locke's letters concerning toleration is that "every one is orthodox to himself" (1983, p.23).[9] The basic and modest point that Locke is making is that to believe something is to believe that it is true. "For whatsoever any Church believes, it believes to be true . . ." (1983, p.23). Hence, Locke argues, there is no effective difference between saying that only magistrates with true religious beliefs should enforce them and saying that all magistrates should enforce their religious beliefs. There is no practical difference between saying that only orthodox princes should impose their favored faith and forms of worship and saying that all princes should impose their favored faith and forms of worship. For, *every* ruler will take himself to be among the true believers, among the orthodox, who have just been told that they may proceed with their impositions. No ruler will think, "I see now that, if only I were among the orthodox, I would be justified in imposing my favorite doctrines and rites." Locke's point, of course, is not to *endorse* all princes enforcing their religious views within their respective realms. Such systematic enforcement would include princes punishing individuals with genuinely true religious convictions and righteous forms of worship for failing to adopt genuinely false beliefs and blasphemous practices. This is repellant even to those who call for the punishment of the heterodox. Moreover, the practical effect of all magistrates taking themselves to be justified in punishing disbelievers is continuous strife and tumult. The point of Locke's claim that everyone is orthodox to himself is that one cannot restrict who will take himself to be justified in imposing his views and punishing dissenters by saying that only the orthodox may do this. Therefore, unrelenting religious warfare and the punishment of those with genuinely true beliefs by those with genuinely false beliefs can only be avoided by rejecting the premise that the orthodox—*whoever they are*—may impose their faith and forms of worship on the heterodox. "[U]ntil this great and fundamental popish doctrine of using force in matters of religion be laid aside there is little hopes of peace, and truth in the world" (1997, p.374).

Upon whom, then, may the orthodox or those who take themselves to be orthodox, that is, everyone, impose their faith and forms of worship? The answer is upon themselves. In their religious endeavors, all who take themselves to be orthodox may dispose of their persons and their possessions—recall the calf—as they respectively see fit. And this universal liberty will be nonconflictual because what is mine and what is thine constitute separate spheres of authority. Neither party's authority extends to control of the other's property; and neither party can claim to be injured by the other party exercising control over his property. As long as each individual is minding his own business, no man's error is prejudicial to any other man. This explains why there is no need at all for the surrender of private judgment in the case of religious belief and practice. Private judgment in religious matters is about how one will dispose of what is one's own in the pursuit of salvation. Thus, each person can act on his own private judgment without interfering with any other person acting on his private judgment. This is in contrast to persons' private judgments about where the boundaries lie between what is mine and what is thine. It is the conflict between those private judgments that cause the inconveniences of the state of nature and require individuals to establish an umpire to make reasonable determinations of where those boundaries lie. No comparable religious umpire is needed.

I have said that the basic and modest point that Locke is making when he says that everyone is orthodox to himself is simply that to believe something is to believe that it is true. Yet, in ways that we cannot trace or untangle here, Locke's claim takes on a more and more skeptical edge. It sounds as though no man can inspect his own religious convictions and determine that they are untrue. It seems that each of us simply has to take *whatever* religious convictions we have to be the truth. Locke makes a variety of pronouncements about what the true religion is. He tells us in short order that it is Christianity, that it is Protestantism, and that it is Anglicanism (1823, p.63 and p.64). He also tells us that the central truth is that "Jesus Christ was put to death at Jerusalem, and rose again from the dead" (1823, p.144). Yet by *A Third Letter* Locke is insisting that no religion is *known* to be true. Although he takes Christianity to be true, "faith it is still, and not knowledge; persuasion, and not certainty" (1823, p.144). Since Locke wants to say that, whatever a magistrate believes, if he is told that he should enforce true belief, he will enforce his own belief, Locke is eager to insist that nothing about the quality of one's belief will undercut one's persuasion. The mark of one's "full persuasion" is not a matter of how good one's reasons are but, rather, one's willingness to venture one's soul upon one's belief (1823, p.145). This feature of Locke's stance leads Proast to charge in his second letter that Locke either believes that there is no true religion or (more likely) believes that "though some one Religion be *the true Religion*, yet no man can have any more reason, than another man of another Religion may have, to believe his to be *the true Religion*." If Locke holds to the latter belief, he

. . . renders it vain and idle to enquire after the true Religion, and only a piece of good luck if any man be of it, and such good luck as he can never know that he has, till he come into the other world. (1984, p.47)

If Proast is correct, then *if* the truth of one's religious convictions still matter, one's salvation or damnation will be entirely a matter of luck; for one cannot direct oneself from false to true beliefs.

In some passages Locke seems to deal with this problem by denying that the truth of one's religious convictions does matter! In *A Letter* Locke backs away from the *Second Treatise* doctrine that he who acts on his private judgment had better be right when he comes before God. Instead, Locke says that God will retribute to each "according to his sincerity and uprightness in endeavoring to promote Piety, and the publick Weal and Peace of Mankind" (1983, p.49). All that seems to matter is sincerity and uprightness. In his *Third Letter*, Locke tells us that religious sin consists in acting against one's religious persuasion. Even though a Jew who becomes a Christian has moved over to the truth, if he still believes that the Messiah is yet to come, then his conversion is "highly criminal." A papist who moves over to the reformed church while still believing that the Roman church is the true one is a "great villain." So, "when all is done, the immediate guide of our actions can be nothing but our conscience, our judgment, and persuasion" (1823, p.147). This is not quite to say that the truth of the persuasion one arrives at does not matter. Yet how could God damn someone for embracing and acting on a false but persuasive religious belief—since it would be sinful for that individual not to embrace and act on it? Note that the more Locke is driven to deny our knowledge of theological propositions, the less sense it makes for him to rely upon such propositions in his inquiries about the law of nature.

It remains only to consider very briefly, the counterproposal that Proast offers in his initial critique of Locke and Locke's response to this counter-proposal. Proast declares his agreement with Locke that force as such cannot produce salvific belief and that severe penalties should not be employed by the magistrate in promoting true religion and proper worship. Nevertheless, he holds that moderate coercion can and should be used to get people "to consider those Reasons and Arguments which are proper and sufficient to convince them, but which, without being forced, they would not consider." In this way, force "*indirectly*" and "*at a distance*" can be of

> ... some service toward the bringing of men to embrace that Truth, which otherwise, either through Carelessness or Negligence they

would never acquaint themselves with, or through Prejudice they would reject and condemn unheard . . . (1984, p.5)

Proast does not tell us very clearly at what point moderate coercion is to be applied. It seems that it should be applied to make individuals "submit to Instruction, and give a fair Hearing to the Reasons which are offer'd, for the enlightning of their minds and discovering the Truth to them." (1984, p.13). Yet often Proast suggests a more general practice of laying penalties on those who deviate from the true religion. Such deviation is a sign that they have been moved by lusts and passions rather than reason; and the prospect of suffering penalties for deviation "may balance the weight of those Prejudices which encline them to prefer a false Way before the True" (1984, p.11). Individuals are not coerced into attending instruction. Rather, according to Proast's second letter, coercion comes in to counteract "the corrupt Nature of Man" which makes "false Religions . . . ever more agreeable than the true" (1984, p.7). The natural allure of false religions is to be counteracted by exposing those who follow them to "Thorns and Briars" (1984, p.10). The result, according to Proast, will be that individuals are more willing to evaluate religions on their rational merits.

Locke brings a barrage of arguments against this counter-proposal. First, there is the argument that derives from the maxim that everyone is orthodox to himself. Proast's claim that only magistrates who hold to the true religion should use force amounts in practice to an invitation to all magistrates to use force to drive people to their own religion. Second, magistrates are, if anything, less likely to have gotten hold of true religion than their subjects—certainly less likely than their subjects would be were all religions allowed to enter the marketplace of religious ideas. Proast rejects Locke's optimism about the truth being able to shift for herself. For, according to Proast's second letter, we must recognize "that blindness which Vice brings upon the Minds of Men." (1984, p.3). Against this Locke argues that the blind might as well lead themselves as be lead by those who are magisterially blind:

If men, apt to be mislead by their passions and lusts, will guard themselves from falling into error by punishments laid on them by men as apt to be mislead by passions and lusts as themselves, how are they safer from falling into error? (1823, pp.178–9)

Third, Locke argues that Proast's proposed scheme is radically misdirected or misdescribed. That scheme calls for penalties to be inflicted upon everyone who is not of the magistrate's church even though many of these people will have already attended (as best they can) to the reasons for subscribing to the magistrate's church; and that scheme calls for no penalties to be inflicted on members of the magistrate's church even though many of them will not have attended to the reasons for subscribing to it. In other words, the scheme pretends to punish people for not attending to reasons but actually punishes people for not being of the magistrate's church (1823, p.74. and p.93.). Fourth, how will Proast know whether or not punishment should be continued? Suppose a dissenter still refuses to conform after being forced to attend to the reasons for the magistrate's religion. The dissenter insists that he has carefully attended and carefully rejected the case for this religion. In contrast, the magistrate insists that his continued non-conformity is evidence that the dissenter has never sufficiently attended. Indeed, why not take the dissenter's ongoing refusal to conform as more and more unambiguous evidence of his unwillingness truly to consider? Proast has "set no time, nor bounds, to this consideration of arguments and reasons, short of being convinced." According to Locke, the real message from Proast to the dissenter is ". . . till you are brought to consider reasons and arguments proper and sufficient to convince you, that is, *till you are convinced*, you are punished on" (1823, p.77, emphasis added).

Part 3

Reception and Contemporary Relevance

The Reception and Philosophical Legacy of Locke's Political Philosophy

I have marshaled textual evidence and philosophical analysis in support of an understanding of Locke as a rights-oriented classical liberal. I have also displayed the strength and depth—as well as some of the shortcomings—of Locke's arguments concerning natural rights, property rights, rights of resistance, and toleration. I begin this concluding chapter with a brief discussion of the enormously complex dispute about what sort and degree of influence Locke's political writings had in the several generations after their publication. The remainder of this chapter examines several central Lockean insights and some Lockean themes that are prominent in contemporary political philosophy. Many of these themes have reemerged in the wake of Robert Nozick's defense of Lockean political theory (1974) and, so, it will often be natural to cast my discussion in terms of a comparison of Locke and Nozick.

The Reception of Locke's Political Thought

The actual historical influence of Locke's political writings is a subject of great controversy among historians of ideas and political movements. I cannot possibly do justice to this difficult topic; but perhaps I can convey a bit of a sense of the debate by commenting briefly on the most central focal point of this controversy, viz., Locke's historical influence on the American Revolution.[1] The old standard view—articulated by Carl Becker in *The Declaration of Independence: A Study in the History of Ideas* (1922)—took Lockean doctrine to be dominant within or soon after the Glorious Revolution and took this dominance to carry over quite directly to the American Revolution. The revisionist views introduced in the

1960s and 1970s portrayed Locke as a largely peripheral figure with respect to both revolutions. The boldest of these revisionist views focuses on what it takes to be a deeply non-Lockean tradition of civic republicanism, which is cast as the primary ideological motivation for both the Glorious and the American Revolutions. As historians such as J. G. A. Pocock conceive it—in, for example, *The Machiavellian Moment* (1975)— this civic republicanism (or civic humanism) was strongly opposed to the rising individualism and commercial character of the modern era and sought a return to a more virtuous, less corrupt, more communitarian, and less enterprising social and political world. The core value for this civic republicanism was the special sort of self-fulfillment which one could only achieve as a citizen actively engaged in political life (Pocock 1975). Other authors—such as Gary Wills in *Inventing America* (1979)— insist that Scottish Enlightenment figures like Francis Hutcheson, with their greater emphasis on man's moral sense and on man's pursuit of happiness, were of much greater influence than Locke.[2] Yet other authors point to the extensive historical-constitutional arguments employed in defense of both the Glorious and the American Revolutions as an indication of their non-Lockean character.

Contrary to this attempted scholarly marginalization of Locke, my cautious judgment is that the correct view is a more nuanced version of the old standard view. The correct view is more nuanced in recognizing the more gradual growth of the influence of Locke's political views[3] and in recognizing that a good deal of what the various revisionist historians point to—for example, the civic republican critique of corruption— actually complements rather than contradicts Locke's own doctrine. Indeed, it is precisely because the core Lockean ideas formed the center of the body of thought that motivated the pro-revolutionary colonists that when Thomas Jefferson set out in the Declaration of Independence to articulate "the American mind" of 1776 by conveying "the harmonizing sentiments of the day, whether expressed in conversation, in letters, printed essays, or the elementary books of public rights, as in Aristotle, Cicero, Locke, Sidny, etc.,"[4] he produced an undeniably Lockean document.

The influence of Locke's political views grew slowly and indirectly in the decades following the Glorious Revolution. Goldie (1980), Ashcraft (1986), and Zuckert (1994) have argued convincingly that Locke's sort of radical Whig doctrine—with its emphasis on natural rights, social contract, limited government, and justified resistance—was only one element within the ideological and political coalition of convenience which supported William against James. Moreover, the *Two Treatises* were published after the Revolution and anonymously. Probably only after Locke's death was it generally known that the *Two Treatises* was the work of the renowned author of the *ECHU*. Perhaps the most widely read statement of radical Whig Lockean theory in the decades after the Revolution was an anonymous pamphlet entitled *Political Aphorisms: Or, the True Maxims of Government Displayed*, very substantial portions of which were lifted word for word and without acknowledgment from the *Second Treatise*. This pamphlet also contains historical-constitutional arguments in support of resistance against unjust authority which were lifted word for word from other contemporary sources and which, as the compiler of *Political Aphorisms* correctly perceived, complement Locke's philosophical arguments.[5] As the alliance of convenience between Whigs and anti-Catholic Tories broke down after the Glorious Revolution and public debate about the basis for legitimate authority and legitimate resistance reignited, expanded versions of this pamphlet were issued—as *Vox Populi, Vox Dei* in 1709 and as *The Judgment of Whole Kingdoms and Nations* in 1710. Among many subsequent editions of this pamphlet were the still anonymous editions published in Philadelphia (1773), Boston (1774), and Rhode Island (1774).[6] *An Argument for Self-Defense* (1710) is another striking example of an anonymous and thoroughly Lockean pamphlet which was issued as ideological debate was re-kindled in the first couple of decades of the eighteenth century. This work is a very intelligent and elegant presentation of Locke's political doctrine which only departs from Locke by openly rejecting the idea that, for the sake of the public good, one must not kill a prince who is merely being unjust to a single person (Anon. 1710, 193)

Locke's influence in the English-speaking world advanced along numerous other paths in the early eighteenth century, for example, through the several English editions—the first being in 1717—of Jean Barbeyrac's edition of Samuel Pufendorf's *On the Law of Nature and Nations*. In this very influential work, Barbeyrac repeatedly contrasted Locke's views to Pufendorf's—to Locke's advantage. Barbeyrac sides with Locke on, for example, the possibility of political power making men worse off than they would be in the state of nature, the existence of an individual right to punish in the state of nature, the acquisition of property rights in the state of nature without need of general consent, and the right of resistance against tyrannical rulers.[7] Perhaps the most important path by which Lockean political thought advanced in England and subsequently in the American colonies was the 1720–1723 newspaper series *Cato's Letters*, authored by John Trenchard and Thomas Gordon (writing as "Cato"), which was republished in many bound editions through the first half of the eighteenth century (Trenchard and Gordon, 1995). *Cato's Letters* is pivotal for the dispute between the civic republican account and the more traditional Lockean account of the motivation of the American revolutionaries because partisans of each account agree on the enormous influence of these *Letters*.[8] Thus, the civic republican interpretation of British Whig thought in the first half of the eighteenth century and of American revolutionary thought in the decades running up to the Revolution depends heavily on the civic republican reading of *Cato's Letters*. For this reason, Michael Zuckert's strong defense of the radical Lockean character of the *Letters* and powerful critique of the civic republican reading (1994, pp. 297–312) profoundly undercuts the general civic republican interpretation. In short, Zuckert shows that *all* the core Lockean theses also form the basis for Cato's libertarian and individualist doctrine and that, with almost perfect consistency, Cato rejects the antilibertarian, anti-individualist, and anticommercial sentiments associated with civic republicanism. As Zuckert and other friends of the Lockean reading of the *Letters* point out, a good deal of what is taken to be anti-Lockean, civic republican sentiment in the *Letters* is simply more detailed expressions of claims that can readily be found in Locke about the allure of political power for those who seek to plunder and enslave others and the susceptibility of political rulers to corrupting flattery and covetousness.

There is little reason, therefore, to recast along civic republican lines the apparently strongly Lockean pronouncements of the American colonists as they argued their way up to and through the Declaration of Independence.[9] Nor is there any reason to see the recurrent appeal to happiness and the Declaration's citation of the pursuit of happiness, rather than the acquisition and enjoyment of property, as the third fundamental natural right—along with life and liberty—as any departure from an essentially Lockean perspective. I do not mean to say that there was anything like intellectual uniformity among the pro-Revolution colonists. Clearly the differences that divided politically minded Americans into Federalists and Anti-Federalists as the Constitution was debated in the late 1780s and into Federalists and Republicans after the Constitution's ratification did not arise out of nothing. Nevertheless, I think the following sampling of pronouncements by colonial opponents of British policy accurately convey the substantially Lockean character of the increasing resistance to British rule.

Writing against British taxation in the mid-1760s, John Dickinson maintained "that we cannot be happy without being free—that we cannot be free without being secure in our property—that we cannot be secure in our property, if, without our consent, others may, as by right, take it away . . ." (Eicholz, 2000, p.24) In 1772, Samuel Adams produced a remarkably perspicacious statement of Lockean political theory—which drew on both the *Second Treatise* and *The Letter Concerning Toleration*—to articulate the rights of the colonists (Adams, 1772). Adams follows Locke all the way from fundamental state of nature rights to resistance and toleration. Perhaps the following passage most directly links Locke with the grounding of the American Revolution:

> In short, it is the greatest Absurdity to suppose it in the Power of one or any Number of Men, at the entering into Society, to renounce their essential Rights, or the Means of preserving those Rights; when the grand End of Civil Government from the very Nature of its Institution, is for the Support, Protection and Defence of those very Rights' The principal of which as is before observed, are *Life, Liberty,* and *Property*. (Adams, 1772, p.265)

In 1773 and in opposition to British taxation of the colonists in, Daniel Leonard wrote:

> That men have a natural right to retain their justly acquired property or dispose of it as they please without injuring others, is a proposition that has never been controverted to my knowledge: That they should lose this right by entering society is repugnant to common sense and the united voice of every writer of reputation upon the subject'.[10] (Leonard quoted Eicholz, 2000, p.37)

One of the documents which Jefferson almost certainly had in mind during his own drafting of the Declaration of Independence as a synoptic statement of the American mind was the Bill of Rights which George

Mason had composed in 1774 for the Virginia constitution according to which

> . . . all men are by nature equally free and independent, and have certain inherent rights, of which, when they enter into a state of society, they cannot by any compact, deprive or divest their posterity; namely, the enjoyment of life and liberty, the means of acquiring and possessing property, and pursuing and obtaining happiness and safety. (Eicholz, 2000, p.43)

Mason's linkage of property and happiness as conditions which each has a right to acquire or pursue is noteworthy because it highlights the fact that for the Lockean colonists—as for Locke himself—there was no conflict between securing rights, including property, and pursuing happiness. Recall here the Lockean doctrine that what people especially need vis-a-vis others in order to attain their comfortable preservation is freedom to dispose as they see fit of their own lives, liberties, and estates. The crucial interpersonal condition for human happiness is liberty. As Cato puts it, perhaps a bit hyperbolically, "liberty is the divine source of all human happiness."

> The privileges of thinking, saying, and doing what we please, and of growing as rich as we can, without any other restriction, than that by all this we hurt not the publick, nor one another, are the glorious privileges of liberty; and its effects, to live in freedom, plenty, and safety. (Trenchard and Gordon 1995, v.1. p.432)

And tyranny is the crucial cause of human misery. In their aversion to human liberty tyrants display

> . . . every-where such constant and strong antipathy to the happiness of mankind, that if there be but one free city within their ken, they are restless in their designs and snares against it . . . There are instances in this age of free cities falling into the claws of tyrants and the miserable difference between their former opulency and their present poorness . . . (Trenchard and Gordon 1995, v.2, p.541)

So, when we find Jefferson invoking a natural right to the pursuit of happiness in the Declaration, we can hardly take this to be a repudiation of the rights of property or of the human value of prosperity.

Let us turn then, finally and very briefly, to a direct comparison of the key theoretical claims which appear near the beginning of the Declaration with core theses of Locke's political doctrine.[11]

(i) ". . . all Men are created equal" and "are endowed by their Creator with certain inalienable Rights" and "among these are Life, Liberty, and the Pursuit of Happiness." This is the Declaration's basic affirmation of men's natural and inalienable rights. All the Declaration explicitly tells us about the grounding of these clearly Lockean rights is that men are endowed with these rights through their creation as moral equals; but it seems reasonable to read this along the lines provided by Mason. Man's original equality is man's original freedom and independence; it is each man's claim against being subject to the will of others.

(ii) ". . . to secure these Rights, Governments are instituted among Men, deriving their just Powers from the Consent of the Governed." Men's basic rights precede the existence of governments (or political societies). Governments (or political societies) are instituted by men in order to better secure those independently obtaining rights. The only just powers which governments possess are those which are conveyed to them for the purpose of the securing of individual rights. Because our most basic rights—for example, to life, liberty, and the pursuit of happiness—are *inalienable*, they cannot be surrendered in the course of establishing governments.

(iii) ". . . whenever any Form of Government becomes destructive of these Ends, it is the Right of the People to alter or abolish it, and to institute new Government, laying its Foundation on such Principles, and organizing its Powers in such Form, as to them shall seem most likely to effect their Safety and Happiness." The primary end, of course, is the securing of men's rights; it is through the securing of that end that people are most likely to attain safety and happiness. When a ruler or a form of government is destructive of those ends, the *people* have a right to resist and replace it with another more suited to serve their ends.

(iv) ". . . Prudence, indeed, will dictate that Governments long established should not be changed for light and transient Causes; and accordingly all Experience hath shewn, that Mankind are more deposed to suffer, while Evils are sufferable, than to right themselves by abolishing the Forms to which they are accustomed." The principle that governments which are destructive of men's rights (and safety and happiness) may be altered or abolished (by extra-legal action) may seem to encourage imprudent opposition based on "light and transient Causes." But such imprudent opposition will not arise because men are, if anything, too slow to resist evil.

(v) "But when a long Train of Abuses and Usurpations, pursuing invariably the same Object, evinces a Design to reduce them under absolute Despotism, it is their Right, it is their Duty, to throw off such Government, and to provide new Guards for their future Security." Resistance is justified when the existing government displays a pattern of action which cannot be construed as merely misguided behavior within the verge of its authority, but rather as conduct that evinces a tyrannical design.

The particular charges which the Declaration then brings against George III are, of course, different from the charges in Locke's *Second Treatise* which were directed against Charles II and James II. Yet they match those former charges by including both complaints about violations of substantive rights—"He has . . . sent hither Swarms of Officiers to harass our People, and eat out their Substance"—and complaints about George's undermining of constitutional structures intended to protect the people's rights—"He has dissolved Representative Houses repeatedly, for opposing with manly Firmness his invasions of the Rights of the People." Moreover, in good Lockean fashion, the Declaration maintains that it is the King, not those now resisting him, who has dissolved the offending regime. "He has abdicated Government here, declaring us out of his Protection and waging War against us."

Individualism and Rights

I turn now to a review of several central Lockean insights and related Lockean themes that are prominent in contemporary political philosophy. At the core of Locke's classical liberalism is his doctrine of natural rights. Rights, especially natural rights, function to protect individuals in their pursuit of their own chosen goals. They morally immunize individuals from interference by others—by freelance criminals, by zealots, or by governments—whether the interfering agents are seeking their own private advantage or what they conceive to be the radiant public good. Rights are the moral bastions on which individuals may take their stand against those who would conscript the right-holders into their own projects and causes. Karl Marx thought that this showed that rights are fundamentally antisocial; they sanction the withdrawal of individuals from all social interaction and accommodation (Tucker, 1978, p.42). Locke understood that this is deeply mistaken. For rights are precisely what enable individuals to discover or create diverse voluntary associations—be they familial, economic, intellectual, or religious—in which people with all their different proclivities can cooperate to mutual advantage. The only coordination among individuals which rights preclude is conscripted, coerced, and, hence, almost always, exploitative and subordinating coordination.

Rights are individualistic in their protection of individuals pursuing their own ends in their own chosen ways. But they are also individualistic in a further and deeper sense. Rights presuppose the *value* or *importance* of individuals pursuing and achieving their own separate, personally valuable, ends. The deeper individualism which rights protect is the separate individualized value which adheres to each person's promotion of his own separate good. It is because each of us has a good of his own—a good to which he, but not others, sensibly devotes himself—that each of us has rights protective of our pursuit of that special personal good. Recognizing persons as right-holders turns on recognizing them each as beings with separate ends of their own which they are rational to promote. For the natural rights which others have against one correspond to the reasonableness of one's being circumspect in one's conduct toward other beings each of whom has rational ends of his own. This is why one of the two crucial facts about our "inborn constitution" from which, according to Locke, our possession of rights is to be inferred is our each having our own happiness (our comfortable preservation) as our separate rational end. The other crucial fact is, of course, the moral equality which exists among us. Although Locke outlines the inborn constitution program in *ELN*, that program cannot get rolling towards protective rights until Locke turns away from the distaste for self-interest that he expresses in *ELN* (pp.127–31) and toward the rationality of each agent's pursuit of his happiness which he expresses in "Morality," "Thus I Think," "Of Ethic in General," and *ECHU*.

Thus, in *Anarchy, State, and Utopia*, the most prominent relatively recent excursion into Lockean theory, Nozick is on the right path when he invokes the separateness of persons as the root idea in the case for protective natural Lockean rights. For the separateness of persons is a normative postulate that includes at least the idea that each individual rationally pursues his own good, his own happiness. That John's happiness is a rational end *for John* does not as such make John's happiness a rational end *for Tom*. Hence, although the value of John's happiness calls upon John to incur costs to promote that happiness, it does not call upon Tom to incur costs to promote that happiness. There is no joint or aggregate happiness to which the individual ought to sacrifice his own happiness. Nozick's view is that this normative separateness of persons *also* makes it impermissible for John or society to *impose* sacrifices upon Tom for the sake of John's happiness or the aggregate happiness or any other purported common and impersonal end:

> The moral side constraints upon what we may do, I claim, reflect the fact of our separate existences. They reflect the fact that no moral balancing act can take place among us; there is no moral outweighing of one of our lives by others so as to lead to a greater overall *social* good. There is no justified sacrifice of some of us for others. (1974, p.33)

Yet Nozick moves very quickly here from the claim that individuals are not obligated to sacrifice their respective good for the sake of any purported societal good to the claim that all individuals have rights against having such sacrifices imposed on them.

Perhaps there is more to Nozick's inference than appears on the surface. Very likely Nozick is thinking that the appropriate basic *interpersonal* norm for a world of individuals each of whom rationally pursues his own good—and, hence, for a world without transpersonal ends which all should serve—must be a norm which *limits the means* by which individuals may pursue their own good and, furthermore, that the natural limitation along these lines is that each being who exists for his own purposes is not to be treated as a means for other people's purposes. Nozick may well also be thinking that one's perfect freedom from moral subordination to the good of others requires *both* that one not be obligated to sacrifice one's good for the good of others *and* that others be obligated not to impose such sacrifices upon one. Lastly, Nozick may well be thinking that each individual's possession of rational ends of his own gives each person a type of standing as an ultimate center of value; and one recognizes that standing in one's conduct toward that person by not treating him as means to one's own ends. In short, Nozick may implicitly be relying upon Locke's false presumption, perfect freedom, and like reason arguments for natural rights. If he is, there is much more to his inference to rights than is commonly recognized.

The Role and Character of Rights

Rights function as devices for resolving interpersonal disputes without recourse to any common measure of what makes actions worthy of performance (Steiner, 1974). They allow us to resolve disputes about how an individual may act without having to agree upon what measure of the worth of a proposed action should be employed and how that action scores on that measure. Recall Locke's discussion of the man who proposes to sacrifice a calf as part of a religious rite. He thinks the action is well-pleasing to God; others disagree about whether it is well-pleasing to God or whether being pleasing to God is the appropriate measure. If the issue is the value of this proposed action (compared to the alternative dispositions of the calf), the dispute will only be settled if we agree both on what measure of value should be employed and what particular assessment that measure yields. Yet, the more diversity of purposes, of substantive moral codes, and of religious views there is among us and the more individualized our ends are, the less possible any such resolution is.

Fortunately, we can resolve such interpersonal disputes by identifying who has *the right* to determine the disposition of the object the use of which is in question rather than by reaching agreement about the worthiness or value of the action in question. The individual who favors the sacrifice of the calf gets to perform that action if and only if it is his calf. A resolution of this sort works by privatizing the decision, that is, by delivering us from the need for a public judgment about how best to use the calf. The privatization of such decisions allows us to live at peace with one another—indeed, to proceed to all sorts of mutually beneficial interactions with one another—despite deep divisions among us about what actions are desirable, noble, or well-pleasing to God. Resolute de-politicalization of decision making rather than a futile search for more enlightened modes of political decision-making is the fundamental Lockean formula for how wider and increasingly diverse ranges of people can peacefully coexist. That privatization of decision-making begins with a recognition of persons as self-owners and proceeds to a recognition of persons' acquired property rights. Peaceful coexistence and the prospect of cooperation to mutual advantage emerge from our identification of what is mine and what is thine.

For Locke, all fundamental rights are forms of property. This is most vividly conveyed by the disposition to describe the rights each individual has with respect to himself as instances of self-ownership or self-propriety. And the crucial thing about property is that, if one has a property in a given object, one gets by one's choice to determine how that object will be employed; one gets to do as one sees fit with that object. Property is the ground of choice and liberty. What is essential to one's right over some object is not that it is in one's interest to possess or dispose of that object but that one has the authority to do so. For this reason, I may have a right to a bottle of whiskey even if, as an alcoholic, it is not in my interest to possess that bottle or to dispose of it in the manner that I am inclined. I may have a right to my body even if I foolishly refuse to allow the most skilled surgeon in the world to remove a dangerous tumor. Thus, as we saw in examining Locke on toleration, the Lockean conception of rights supports a strong and principled anti-paternalism. The correlative for Locke of this radical freedom from the coercive interference of others is that each person is responsible himself for judging how he will conduct his life. No one should pretend that others will be able successfully to judge for one. No one benefits from such a pretense except, according to Locke, those who seek power over one.[12]

Property Rights and Prosperity

According to Locke, private property both in its narrow and broad sense is also the basis for prosperity. Property in one's person and one's labor is essential for the establishment of property in the fruits of one's labor; and property in the fruits of one's labor and in what one receives *in exchange* for the fruits of one's labor—including the *money* one may receive for one's labor or for the fruits of that labor—is crucial both to one's capacity to plan one's economically productive activities and to one's having incentive to plan and carry out those activities. Since almost all wealth derives from human industry, that is, from the development and deployment of human talent and energy, the key to growing prosperity is the encouragement of human industry. Money greatly magnifies the incentives that individuals have to enhance and exercise their productive capacities in ways that will satisfy the demand for goods or services which individuals will create through their own enhancement and exercise of their productive capacities. Even more importantly, money radically increases the range over which mutually beneficial trade takes place. More and more people benefit in more different sorts of ways from entering the market—both as producers and consumers—with their distinctive resources, talents, knowledge, and preferences. As Locke sees it, the entire process is a huge positive sum interaction. The gains are so great that even if considerably more inequality of wealth arises in the process, all can gain from participation in it. The other side of the incentive story is that effective protection of people's property rights, that is, effective defense against or punishment of enslavers, thieves, and defrauders, radically diminishes people's incentive to attempt to gain by preying upon their fellows. The enforcement of property rights channels individuals away from zero or negative sum interaction, that is, predation and plunder, and into positive sum interaction, that is, production and trade.

A Hobbesian sovereign with unlimited legal authority might appreciate all of these Lockean points; and, recognizing that his interests are served by the peace and prosperity of his realm, he might well *decree* private property rights to exist. He might much more specifically decree that each individual has legal (enacted) rights over his own person, over his labor, over the fruits of his labor, and over whatever he gets in voluntary exchange for the fruits of his labor. Indeed, Hobbes may well have thought that the appearance of an absolute and unlimited sovereign was mankind's best bet for attaining such legal rights. Albeit, as Hobbes himself insisted, these legal rights, as manifestations of the will of the sovereign, will always be subject to modification or annulment at the will of the sovereign (1994, II, xxix, 9 and 10). Similarly, a utilitarian who accepts the claims about the social benefits of private property might support the creation of legal rights to private property while denying that these rights are at all grounded in pre-legal, natural rights. What is the Lockean response to such proposals to reap the benefits of private property rights without the burden of grounding legal rights in pre-legal, moral rights?

Part of that response is the conceptual claim that it makes no sense to say that one has a property right to an object if the legislative power may take that object from one without one's consent Locke (1980, II, 138). Yet if one's "right" to the object is created by the will of the legislative body, then that "right" can equally well be annulled by the will of that

body, that is, without one's consent. Close to this conceptual claim is
Locke's interesting argument that a sovereign legislator who decrees
that his or its subjects have various "rights" and even protects those
subjects in those "rights" so as best to advance his or its ends no more
recognizes the special moral standing of his or its human subjects than a
farmer recognizes the special moral standing of his animals when he
keeps them from damaging one another. The supreme legislator's
conferring of such legal rights on its subjects

> . . . is no more than what every man, who loves his own power, profit,
> or greatness, may and naturally must do, keep those animals from
> hurting, or destroying one another, who labour and drudge only for
> his pleasure and advantage; and so are taken care of, not out of any
> love the master has for them, but love of himself, and the profit they
> bring him. (1980, II, 93)

Presumably the utilitarian is as guilty of this failure of moral recognition
as the self-interested (Hobbesian) legislator; for the former protects his
subjects for the sake of the general utility that they serve.

Moving from the conceptual to the practical, Locke adds that

> . . . a man's *property* is not at all secure, tho' there be good and equita-
> ble laws to set the bounds of it between him and his fellow subjects, if
> he who commands those subjects have power to take from any private
> man, what part he pleases of his *property*, and use and dispose of it as he
> thinks good. (1980, II, 138)

The agency against which individuals most need protective rights is
the supreme legislative body; but "rights" granted to individuals by such
a body will provide no protective fences against that body's will. Speaking
even more practically, the supreme legislative body—whoever or whatever it is—will be strongly motivated to use that power not to advance the
interests of its subjects at large but, rather, to advance its more narrowly
understood interests. Recall here that the proposal under consideration
is to substitute the will of the legislative body for principles of natural
justice; hence, there are no principles of natural justice around even to
guide the legislative body. Nor will considerations of rational prudence
reliably divert a sovereign legislature from engaging in the negative-sum
game of predation upon its subjects. For given the unique power of the

sovereign body, this may be a winning game for it; and even if it is not a winning game, the sovereign body may be so "corrupted with flattery" as to think it is (1980, II, 91).

Of course, the utilitarian supporter of the creation of a Lockean-looking system of legal property rights can insist that his utilitarian sovereign will be morally constrained to serve and protect such a system on the basis of its (presumed) utility. This is not a view that Locke himself addresses. But I think we can make a good guess about what Locke's response would be (beyond, of course, reaffirming the existence of a law of nature to which created legal rights must conform). That response would be that a supreme legislative body will be resolute in serving and protecting such a system of legal rights only if it or the citizenry at large believes that those legal rights are articulations of pre-legal, moral rights—rights which are to be respected even when it looks as though their violation will be socially beneficial. Even if it will not be truly socially advantageous to depart from a Lockean-looking system of legal rights, calculations in terms of social benefits will often *appear* to call for such a departure; and the legislature will resist such calls only if it or the citizenry at large think there are principled reasons for resisting the siren call of social utility.[13] So, on Locke's behalf and against the proposal that we can get the social benefits of a Lockean-looking system of legal rights without the burden of belief in natural rights, I offer F. A. Hayek's contention that:

> The preservation of a free system is so difficult precisely because it requires a constant rejection of measures which appear to be required to secure particular [beneficial] results, on no stronger grounds than that they conflict with a general rule, and frequently without our knowing what will be the costs of not observing the rule in the particular instance . . . Freedom will prevail only if it is accepted as a general principle whose application to particular instances requires no justification. (1973, p.61)

That freedom *is* justified as a general principle is the conclusion of the Lockean arguments which I describe in Chapters 2 and 3. We cannot go beyond that discussion in this concluding chapter.

However, within this discussion of property rights it will be profitable once again briefly to compare Locke with Nozick. Nozick, like Locke, wants to invoke self-ownership on behalf of agents having rights to the fruits of their labor and the receipts of their trades—rights which do not depend upon their being socially useful or their being conferred by legislative will. Yet Nozick is uneasy about Locke's labour-mixing account of the generation of private property rights. So he adopts an argumentative strategy which he thinks will get him to Lockean conclusions without having to *rely* upon the labour-mixing account of just initial acquisitions. Nozick puts on the table his own historical entitlement theory of justice in holdings. According to that theory:

  (i) Individuals can obtain property rights to previously unowned portions of nature through certain modes of acquiring those portions of nature;
 (ii) Individuals can obtain property rights to already acquired objects by receiving them through certain modes of voluntary transfer from their previous owners; and
(iii) Individuals have property rights to whatever they have come to hold in virtue of any concatenation of these two sorts of process (1974, pp.150–3).[14]

The crucial feature of this essentially Lockean doctrine of justice in holdings is that justice in holdings does not require that any preordained pattern or profile of holdings obtain among individuals. *Whatever* pattern or profile of holdings arises among individuals who obtain possessions in accordance with the specified procedures will be just. Nozick then claims that all (significant) competitors to his historical entitlement conception do specify a pattern or profile of possessions that must obtain for justice to be satisfied. Hence, if he can reasonably reject any conception of justice in holdings which does demand that such a pattern or profile obtain, he can conclude that all competitors to his historical entitlement have been eliminated.

   Rather than consider in general all competing conceptions, let us focus on the specific competing conception which Nozick is most concerned to reject. This is John Rawls' difference principle which says that taxes and transfer payments are to be arranged so that those on the lowest economic rung in society end up with as much income as it is possible to provide to individuals on the lowest rung (1971, pp.75–83). Rawls' presumption is that to maximize the income that flows to the lowest-income individuals the more talented and energetic members of society should be allowed to retain enough (and only enough) of what they produce to keep them producing; all the rest of their product should be transferred (minus administrative expenses) to members of the least advantaged class. Nozick's response is that any such *system* makes the members of the least advantaged class the partial owners of the more talented and energetic individuals. And *that* is unacceptable because, *as Locke has taught*, all individuals are self-owners. (Notice that the solicitude shown to these more talented and energetic individuals is like the solicitude the master shows toward his useful animals.) If, as Nozick would maintain, all significant competitors to the historical entitlement conception do to some degree make some individuals the partial owners of others, then given the principle of self-ownership, all significant competitors are eliminated.

Yet, why is it that, for example, the difference principle institutes partial ownership over the talented and energetic? The tax collector merely shows up and trucks off x percent of the corn which Tom has grown and harvested and y percent of beef that John has raised and cured. The system institutes its ownership (or the ownership of the least advantaged) over that seized corn and beef. But on what basis can it be said that *this* amounts to instituting partial ownership of Tom and John? It seems that the only basis for saying this is that something which is included in Tom's and in John's self-ownership, viz., their respective labor, is invested in their respective products. But, then, Nozick's conclusion that conceptions of justice like Rawls' call for the institution of partial ownership of some *persons* by others depends upon the Lockean thesis which he seeks not to rely upon, viz., that persons acquire rights to their products in virtue of their investment of their labor in those products.

It has also been Nozick's discussion of Locke which reinvigorated philosophical examination of Locke's enough and as good proviso. Yet Nozick's own discussion is unsatisfying because he never makes clear what precisely is the basis for limiting the rights of property holders. Why may the apparently rightful holder of the only water hole in a vast desert *not* exclude from his property the wanderer who, dying of thirst, stumbles toward the water hole? Is it because on some level or to some degree the water hole really is the common property of all mankind? We have noticed that Locke may have a quite different explanation for why the wanderer may not be rightfully excluded. That explanation goes back to the basal liberty of self-preservation. It is precisely because each individual has this liberty that there can be no common right to the earth which excludes individuals from life-sustaining acts of use and appropriation.

The permissibility of the initial appropriation of the water hole depends upon this liberty of self-preservation. But, in turn, it seems that when the wanderer subsequently stumbles toward the water hole, in virtue of *his* liberty of self-preservation, we cannot construe the present owner's right to the water hole as blocking the wanderer's life-sustaining action.

Consent and State Legitimacy

Although Locke is eager to hold that property rights are not based upon universal consent and is eager to say that the initial establishment of political authority does not require that everyone in the region of that authority consent to it, he still holds that any regime's authority over any given individual requires the authorizing consent of that individual. Since Locke wants to hold that some regimes, for example, the regime of William and Mary, are owed obedience by all of its subjects, he needs to appeal to tacit consent to bring all those subjects under an obligation to obey the law. But as we have seen (Chapter 4, third section), the appeal to tacit consent makes almost every government one which exists with the consent of the governed.

Could Locke have found a route to state legitimacy which does *not* run through general consent? After all, John's consent is not needed for Tom to be morally free to enforce the law of nature against John. If, in the state of nature, John makes off with Tom's cow, Tom has every right to round up a posse and come after John. Tom and his companions may with justifiable force require that John return the cow or make reparations to Tom; and he and his companions may impose punishment on John as long as it is no more than is necessary "to make it an ill bargain to the offender, give him cause to repent, and terrify others from doing the like" (1980 II, 12). Suppose that Tom and his posse remain at the ready. They develop some expertise at enforcing the law of nature whenever any of their rights are violated or whenever such a violation is imminent. Out of goodwill or just to keep in practice, they defend the rights of neighbors who are not themselves members of the posse and extract reparation payments and impose permissible punishments on violators of their neighbors' rights. Perhaps they get so good at cost-effectively enforcing people's rights via acts of defense, reparation extraction, or punishment that they begin to *sell* this service to people.

Let us continue a bit further this projection of how rights might be secured within a Lockean state of nature. To make clear to its members, employees, and customers when it can be expected to use force and how much force, the Posse, Inc. announces what norms it will enforce and how much it will punish violations of those norms. It announces, for example, that it will enforce the norms "do not use harmful force against any peaceful individual" and "do not seize the fruits of any other person's labor." And it announces punishments for violations of these norms which do not exceed Locke's limits on justifiable punishment. In short, the Posse, Inc. announces standards and measures which all accord with the law of nature. The effect of what they do is that "The law of nature [is] drawn closer, and have by human laws known penalties annexed to them, to inforce their observation" (1980, II, 135). A good number of people who previously were exercising their rights to act as executors of the law of nature now authorize Posse, Inc. to act on their behalf. This is partially because of its efficiency and partially because Posse, Inc. has developed a better reputation for staying within the bounds of the law of nature than those individuals themselves have. Clients of Posse, Inc. are, therefore, less likely to be viewed with suspicion than freelance rights enforcers. Seizing upon the business model pioneered by Posse, Inc., other entrepreneurs form Liberty, Inc., which offers to enforce its customers' state of nature rights more quickly and at a lower price than that charged by Posse, Inc. Aware that overt conflict would be bad for business and would drive potential customers to yet other rights-enforcement firms, Posse, Inc. and Liberty, Inc. agree to standardize their formulations of what norms will be enforced, by what procedures, and with what punishments. They agree on systems of arbitration (e.g., appeals courts) to settle disputes between them about the appropriate norms, procedures, and punishments.

Nobody has any Lockean based complaint against being subjected to the law-enforcement activities of Posse, Inc. or Liberty, Inc. or the confederation which they may form. For none of these agencies are doing anything which would be wrong for any individual to do as an executer of the law of nature in the state of nature. Thus, we have a "rise" of agencies which perform the function which Locke assigns to government. We have the appearance of Lockean umpires whose decisions are based on known and legitimate law and are backed by force. Yet we get this outcome without anything like a social contract (and without the creation of "political society"). Perhaps lots of individuals will sign service contracts with one or another of the rights-enforcement agencies; but these individuals do not compact *with one another* to transfer their executive rights to "political society" or to those agencies. Moreover, there would be no compact *among individuals* to pay for a share of rights-enforcing activities. For it is by way of each individual's service agreement that this individual becomes bound to pay for enforcement services. The tale of Posse, Inc. and Liberty, Inc. is, of course, the tale which the Lockean *anarchist* tells about how the inconveniences of the state of nature could be overcome *within* the state of nature, that is, without establishing *political* authority. Nozick's basic response to this anarchist scenario is that the confederation which these rights-enforcing agencies will form will (or should) evolve into a minimal Lockean state (1974, pp.54–119). The important point here is not whether Nozick or the anarchist is correct about whether a *state* will arise through the processes they envision. Rather, it is that both the Lockean anarchist and the Lockean Nozick agree that no social contract is needed to legitimate institutions which fulfill the purpose of the Lockean state. This is a welcome result for the overall Lockean project; for it allows that project to bypass its weakest link, viz., Locke's doctrine of consent.[15]

Nevertheless, precisely because both the Lockean anarchist and Nozick take the obligation of the individual to pay for protective services to be based on his individual contract with some protective institution, their dispute highlights a problem for *all* Lockeans which Locke himself did not recognize. This problem arises because the benefits generated by rights-protecting institutions are not easily confined to those who voluntarily pay for their services. Therefore, even individuals who benefit from those activities may not willingly agree to pay for them. For these individuals may hope that others will pay and they will get to free ride on these payments by others.

Consider the standard example of national-scale defense against predatory foreign governments. Such defense will tend to benefit all the individuals in the protected territory. So each individual in that territory will anticipate that, if that defense is provided, he will receive that benefit whether or not he has voluntarily agreed to pay for it. Hence, these individuals will have an incentive *not* to contract to pay for this beneficial protective service. The prospect of others' voluntary payment provides one with an incentive *not* to make a reciprocal payment. (Nor, it seems, will rational apprehension of others' rights move one towards payment; for others, it seems, do *not* have rights that one join them in funding the commonly beneficial endeavor.) The result may be that, for lack of funding, the protective service will not get produced (or will be underproduced) and everyone's rights will go unprotected (or under-protected). Although Locke does not realize it, he himself faces a parallel difficulty. For each individual in the state of nature may well ask himself: Why should *I* join political society at the cost of subjecting myself to taxation rather than hold back and hope to enjoy most of the benefits of political society being established *and paid for* by others?

The problem for all Lockeans is that it may be that only by infringing to some degree on individuals' property rights by *coercing* those individuals into paying for rights-enforcing services will those services exist to protect *each* of those individuals against more extensive infringements on their rights. Perhaps the problem is only apparent. Perhaps enough individuals can be induced *noncoercively* to pay enough for those services that they will be adequately funded.[16] But suppose that it is not possible to induce enough individuals to pay enough voluntarily to finance these activities. Then it seems that the Lockean will have to decide whether some violations of the property rights of individuals are to be allowed in order to finance rights-enforcing services which will protect *each* of those individuals against more extensive violations of their rights.[17]

An interesting thought is that Locke's underlying liberty of self-preservation may come into play to explain why, if it is necessary to take some holdings from individuals without their agreement in order to finance such rights enforcing services, those takings will *not* count as violations of the *rights* of those individuals. Recall the two earlier deployments of this moral liberty. The first deployment was against construing the original common ownership of the earth as requiring that each individual get everyone else's consent before he uses or appropriates any natural material. The argument was that this could not be a correct interpretation of the original common ownership of the earth because, under this interpretation, original common ownership would clash with the liberty of self-preservation. The second deployment was in support of the enough and as good proviso. The argument was that the water hole owner's private rights over the water hole cannot be correctly interpreted as requiring the desert wanderer to sit at the edge of the water hole and die of dehydration. For, the desert wanderer is at least at liberty to enter and slake his thirst and, hence, the water hole owner at least does not have a right to exclude the wanderer. Consider now a third deployment of the right to self-preservation. Individuals set out to secure their self-preservation by establishing rights-enforcing institutions. But they discover (let us suppose) that, if the property rights of individuals are interpreted to preclude individuals being coerced to pay for those institutions, those institutions will not get funded and, hence, individuals will not be at liberty to secure their self-preservation. Since the correct interpretation of private property rights must render those rights consistent with the underlying liberty of self-preservation, the correct interpretation of private property rights must allow protective institutions to require private owners to contribute to the funding of those protective institutions—*if (and only if)* those required payments are *necessary* to finance those institutions and the funded institutions protect *each of those individuals from more extensive incursions upon their persons or possessions.*

Note that even this last deployment of the liberty of self-preservation does not confer on the state or state-like protective institutions any function beyond that of protecting the rights of individuals to their lives, liberties, and possessions. These rights are recognized, articulated, and drawn closer—not granted or bestowed—by the codes adopted by state or state-like protective institutions. Hence, these rights stand as moral fences against the conduct of those institutions. The measure of an action's permissibility always remains the rights of those subjected to the action, not the will of the posturing prince. Actions by princes or their minions that trespass upon people's rights are as criminal as the trespassing actions of freelance murderers, ruffians, and thieves. We should never be impressed by mere badges of authority or fooled by our rulers' pretenses. "The injury and the crime is equal, whether committed by the wearer of a crown, or some petty villain. The title of the offender, and the number of his followers, make no difference in the offence, unless it be to aggravate it" (1980, II, 176).

Notes

Chapter 1: The Historical and Ideological Context of Locke's Political Philosophy

[1] I speak here of *individuals* and the rights of *individuals*. But seventeenth century authors spoke of *men* and the rights of *men*; and this was not merely a matter of alternative terminology. For, despite the obvious existence of female monarchs, they all tended to think of *men* as the primary agents and subjects in political life. However, since it would be awkward at best to continually move back and forth between benighted seventeenth century and enlightened twenty-first century terminology, I will often stick with the benighted terminology.

[2] The standard scholarly edition is Locke 1960. Because the punctuation and spelling for the *Second Treatise* in Locke 1980 is less archaic, I have used it for quotations from sections of the *Second Treatise*. Quotations from the *First Treatise* are from Locke 1960.

[3] For a highly accessible and engaging outline of the ideological and political conflicts of this period, see the lecture outlines posted by Johann Sommerville at http://faculty.history.wisc.edu/Sommerville/123/contents.htm.

[4] A detailed case for Locke's involvement in the revolutionary projects of Shaftsbury and the radical Whigs is made in Ashcraft 1986.

[5] See Sidney 1995 and Tyrrell 1681.

[6] I emphasize that this is a simplified presentation of Hobbes—adequate to set the stage for Locke's reaction to Hobbes.

[7] Yet, the naturally individualist men who Hobbes depicts *cannot* forego private judgments on behalf of their private purposes. For every man can pursue only what he himself takes to serve his own good. Thus, men cannot surrender their right to resist 'wounds, and chains, and imprisonment." (1994, II, xiv, 8) Even justly convicted murderers remain at liberty to resist with deadly force their own execution. (1994, II, xiv, 29) Since a right to refuse to do what the sovereign commands if obedience threatens one's good means nothing if the *sovereign's* judgment determines whether obedience threatens one's good, each individual's reserved right to refuse to do what threatens his own good must include each individual's right to judge for himself whether obedience threatens his good. As is often noted, this persistence of private judgment threatens to unravel Leviathan.

Chapter 2: Natural Freedom, Natural Law, and Natural Rights

[1] See also Locke (1959, II, pp.474–5).
[2] This doctrine was well-expressed in the infamous 1579 treatise, *Vindiciae, Contra Tyrannos* (Lanquet and Mornay, 1994, 99).

> Certainly, whatever God wishes is just, and is so simply because He wishes it. But whatever the king wishes ought to be just prior to his wishing it. For nothing is just because the king has sanctioned it, but a king is just who orders to be sanctioned what is just in itself.

[3] The naturalness of Filmer's patriarchalism dissolves if it turns out that paternal authority exists because God decrees it to exist.
[4] See the passage from "Of Ethic in General" presented above and the last paragraph of that fragment (Locke 1997, p.304).
[5] Emphasis added. The last clause does not weaken my point. One would have a *duty* to submit to punishment because one would have violated a norm which is obligatory in virtue of its being a dictate of reason.
[6] See also the opening lines of "Of Ethic in General" (Locke 1997, p.298).
[7] See also (Locke 1998, I, 57).
[8] Locke also likes the workmanship argument because it undercuts *Adam's* authority over other human beings. See (1960, I, 53). For a parallel use of God's authority over us to block the possibility of the transfer of authority from us to an earthly sovereign, see Ferguson (1689, p.6).
[9] In the *First Treatise*, Locke suggests that we can distinguish between what rights a person has with respect to God and what rights he has with respect to other men (1960, I, 39).
[10] See *First Treatise* (1960, I, 67).
[11] The most prominent advocate of this interpretation is A. John Simmons (1992). According to Simmons, Locke endorses a type of rule-consequentialism in which the norms which govern human conduct are those general compliance with which will maximize aggregate human preservation.
[12] *First Treatise*, (Locke 1960, I, 92). See also sections 131 and 134. Locke's friend, James Tyrrell, composed a lengthy critique of Filmer—*Patriarcha Non Monarcha* (1681)—at more or less the same time as Locke was drafting the *Two Treatises*. Tyrrell's treatise is studded with statements like "the great Law of Nature [ordains] that every man ought to endeavour the common good of Mankinde . . . ," (p.17) and Tyrrell *never* goes on to parse this duty in terms of not subordinating, harming, or invading the rights of others. This makes all the more significant Locke's frequent parsing in terms of respect for rights. Tyrrell, *unlike Locke*, goes on to expatiate on the virtue of laying down one's life for the public good (pp.116–17).
[13] In *The First Treatise* (1960, pp.474–5), Locke tries to sustain a contrast between two sorts of reason by distinguishing between two calculations of

interest—one dealing with natural rewards and punishments and one dealing with divine rewards and punishments. But the latter appeal to God's rewards and punishments still reduces the reasonableness of respect for others' rights to its (eternal) happiness payoff. The reason to respect others' rights is not grounded in their nature. Appropriately at this point Locke speaks of "divine law" rather than "natural law."

Chapter 3: More State of Nature Rights

[1] These limitations are first labeled "provisos" in Nozick (1974, pp.174–82).
[2] See the discussion of pulling down the conductive house to prevent yet other houses from burning in chapter 4 and the discussion of choosing between the children of the unjust aggressor and the victor who seeks reparations in chapter 5.
[3] As late as the fragment "Morality" Locke relies upon a consent argument (Locke 1997, p.268). The workmanship argument for men's rights to the fruits of their labor only emerges after Locke learns from Filmer that he cannot give a consent argument for private property.
[4] The classic article is Demsetz (1967).
[5] If John loves the odor of putrefying venison, does his holding on to it until it rots violate the spoilage proviso?
[6] That the existence of things with economic value depends almost entirely on the exercise of human capital is consistent with value attaching to those things because of people's desires for them. See "Venditio" in which Locke essentially takes economic value to be *established by* market price (1997, pp.339–43).
[7] See "For a General Naturalisation" (Locke 1997, pp.322–6) in which Locke argues that one does not have to worry about this immigration driving wages down because when wages drop (significantly) people will stop immigrating.
[8] Yet, later in the *Second Treatise*, he recognizes that native Americans had money—"wamponpeke" (Locke 1980, II, p.184).
[9] This way is suggested by Nozick (1974, p.77). For a different account of a reasonable Lockean proviso, see Mack (2002a, pp.99–103) and (2002b, pp.245–51).
[10] Locke does not question whether *existing* property really is rightful property by the standards which he himself lays out.
[11] In his *Pariarcha non Monarcha*, Tyrrell maintains that parents may put their children to work to cover in part the costs of their obligation to breed them up (1681, p.19).

Chapter 4: From the State of Nature to the State

[1] See also Locke (1980, II, 75).
[2] See also Locke (1980, II, 130).

3   Although individuals authorize political society to act as the defender of their rights, they reserve the right to use their own force in their own defense when no public defender is on the scene.

4   A more extended attempt to work out this solution can be found in Penington (1999).

5   For Locke, the task of providing determinate articulations of the law of nature falls entirely on the *legislature*. Locke seems to have little or no appreciation for the ways in which custom and judicial decision can generate legal norms which resolve disputes about rights. Locke's belief that established law has to be *legislation* reflects his general voluntarist view that law requires a self-conscious and willful law maker.

6   I slide past, as does Locke, the issue of who counts as an adult individual. Are women included in this group? Are servants? Surely Locke wants to say women and servants are subject to the law.

7   Unfortunately in the *Second Treatise* (1980, 243) Locke repeats the unqualified claim that no member of political society can dissolve his tie by his own choice.

Chapter 5: Conquest, Resistance, and Dissolution

1   This conception of law that was advanced in the seventeenth century by the English jurists Edward Coke and Matthew Hale is strongly defended by Hayek (1973).

2   The argument that Locke presents for the prince's immunity also extends executive prerogative beyond the limits defended by Locke in his chapter "Of Prerogative."

3   It's hard to believe that "republic" slipped in accidentally; for this is the only place the word appears in the *Two Treatises*.

4   The reference, of course, is to the scheme of Charles II and especially James II to reintroduce or even reimpose Catholicism.

5   See the fourth section on "Consent and State Legitimacy" in Chapter 7.

6   The invocation of Jeptha (or Jephtha) is odd. For Jephtha is mostly known for having kept his promise to God to sacrifice the first living creature to enter his home after his military victory—which turned out to be his daughter (Judges 11.27).

Chapter 6: Locke on Toleration

1   In Locke (1997), Goldie provides a small extract (pp.372–5) from this unpublished joint work that is generally labeled "'Critical Notes' on Edward Stillingfleet's *Mischief of Separation*."

2   In Locke (1823), the *Second Letter* occupies pp.59–137, the *Third Letter* (pp.138–546), and the unfinished *Fourth Letter* (pp.546–74).

³ On the Locke-Proast exchange, see Vernon (1997). Jeremy Waldron maintains that Proast gets the better of the exchange in Waldron (1988).
⁴ In these summary statements the complicating middleman of Locke's doctrine—political society—drops out.
⁵ See Locke (1980, II), chapter VI.
⁶ Locke adds that, if some disease has wiped out most of the cattle, the magistrate can prohibit cattle from being killed so as to restore the stock. Perhaps this is another case of Locke's willingness to sacrifice liberty for the sake of national wealth.
⁷ Recall the individuation of the rational pursuit of happiness which Locke advocates in the *ECHU* (1959, II, p.341).
⁸ Also see Locke's *Third Letter* (1823, pp.166–7).
⁹ See also (1983, p.32). A striking indication of Locke's attachment to this point is that it is reiterated in the last paragraph of his unfinished *Fourth Letter* (1823 pp.573–4).

Chapter 7: The Reception and Philosophical Legacy of Locke's Political Philosophy

¹ I am grateful to Hans Eicholz for his guidance through some of the scholarship on the ideological origins of the American Revolution. Eicholz (2001) provides a comprehensive critical discussion of the many ways in which the American Revolution has been depicted as non-Lockean—or even anti-Lockean.
² For a decisive refutation of Wills, see Hamowy (1979).
³ There were a total of 18 printings of the *Two Treatises* in Britain between 1689 and 1779. The first American printing (of the *Second Treatise*) was in Boston in 1773. See Locke (1960, pp.121–5).
⁴ Thomas Jefferson to Henry Lee, May 8, 1825 (Petersen 1984, 1501).
⁵ Another 1690 pamphlet, *The Fundamental Constitution of the British Government*, endorses Locke's philosophical stance while chiding Locke for not also supplying the supporting historical-constitutional argument. See Atwood (1690).
⁶ For a detailed discussion of *Political Aphorisms*, see Ashcraft and Goldsmith 1983. Early English Books Online still lists this pamphlet as a work of Locke.
⁷ See the selections from Barbeyrac in Goldie (1999, volume 2, 262–82).
⁸ See the "Introduction" to Trenchard and Gordon (1995), xxxiv–xxxvii.
⁹ The prologue of Zuckert (1994) provides an overview of recent scholarship on the level of awareness of Locke's *Two Treatises* in colonial America. See pp.18–25.
¹⁰ Subsequently Leonard abandoned both his Lockeanism and his opposition to British rule.
¹¹ See the similar comparison in the prologue of Zuckert (1994).
¹² We must not forget Locke's view that, alongside my right over my life vis-a-vis other men, there is God's right over my life.

[13] Perhaps Lockean-like legal rights could be made more secure by conferring them on the constitutional, rather than the merely statutory, level.

[14] I omit Nozick's principle of rectification.

[15] See the third section of Chapter 4.

[16] See Schmidtz (1991) chapters 1, 4, and 5.

[17] See Mack (1986).

Bibliography

A comprehensive John Locke Bibliography now exists online at: www.libraries. psu.edu/tas/locke/#ls (accessed on December 14, 2008)

Adams, Samuel. (1772), *A State of the Rights of the Colonists.* Reprinted in Goldie (1999), v.3. 265–68.

Anonymous. (1690), *Political Aphorisms: Or the True Maxims of Government Displayed.* Reprinted in Goldie 1999, v.1. 1–32.

Anonymous. (1710), *An Argument for Self-Defense.* Reprinted in Goldie (1999), v.2. 189–198.

Ashcraft, Richard. (1986), *Revolutionary Politics and Locke's Two Treatises of Government.* Princeton: Princeton University Press.

Ashcraft, Richard and Goldsmith, M. M. (1983), "Locke, Revolution Principles, and the Formation of Whig Ideology," *The Historical Journal* 26, 4, 773–800.

Atwood, William. (1690), *The Fundamental Constitution of the English Government.* Extract reprinted in Goldie (1999), v.1. 33–50.

Becker, Carl. (1922), *The Declaration of Independence: A Study in the History of Ideas.* New York: Harcourt Brace & Co.

Buckle, Stephen. (1991), *Natural Law and the Theory of Property.* Oxford: Clarendon University Press.

Colman, John. (1983), *John Locke's Moral Philosophy.* Edinburgh: Edinburgh University Press.

Cranston, Maurice. (1985), *John Locke: A Biography.* Oxford: Oxford University Press.

Demsetz, Harold. (1967), "Toward a Theory of Property Rights," *American Economic Review* 62, 347–59.

Dworetz, Steven. (1990), *The Unvarnished Doctrine.* Durham, NC: Duke University Press.

Eicholz, Hans. (2001), *Harmonizing Sentiments: The Declaration of Independence and the Jeffersonian Idea of Self government.* New York: Peter Lang.

Ferguson, Robert. (1689), "A Brief Justification of the Prince of Orange's Descent into England." London: J.S. Available electronically in Early English Books Online http://libezp.lib.lsu.edu/login?url=http://gateway.proquest. com/openurl?ctx_ver=Z39.88-2003&res_id=xri:eebo&rft_val_fmt=&rft_ id=xri:eebo:image:109506 (accessed December 14, 2008).

Filmer, Robert. (1991), *Filmer: Patriarcha and Other Writings.* Johann Sommerville (ed.) Cambridge: Cambridge University Press.

Goldie, Mark. (1980), "The Revolution of 1689 and the Structure of Political Argument," *Bulletin of Research in the Humanities* 83, 473–564.

— (1991), "The Theory of Religious Intolerance," in Ole Peter Grell, Jonathan I. Israel, and Nicolas Tyache (eds.), *From Persecution to Toleration: The Glorious Revolution and Persecution in England*. Oxford: Clarendon Press, 331–68.

— (1993), "John Locke, Jonas Proast and Religious Toleration 1688-1692," in John Walsh, Colin Hayden, and Stephen Taylor (eds.), *The Church of England c1688-c1833*. Cambridge: Cambridge University Press, 143–71.

— (ed.) (1999). *The Reception of Locke's Politics*. London: Pickering and Chatto.

Grotius, Hugo. (2005), *The Rights of War and Peace*. Indianapolis: Liberty Fund, Inc.

Hamowy, Ronald. (1979), "Jefferson and the Scottish Enlightenment," *William and Mary Quarterly*, 3d series, 31, 503–23.

— (1990), "*Cato's Letters*, John Locke and the Republican Paradigm," *History of Political Thought*, 11, 273–94.

Hayek, Friedrich A. (1973), *Law, Legislation, and Liberty* vol.1. Chicago: University of Chicago Press.

Hobbes, Thomas. (1928), *The Elements of Law*. Ferdinand Tonnies (ed.) Cambridge: Cambridge University Press.

— (1994), *Leviathan*. E. Curley (ed.) Indianapolis: Hackett Publishing.

— (1998), *On the Citizen*. Richard Tuck and Michael Silverthorne (eds) Cambridge: Cambridge University Press.

Huyler, Jerome. (1995), *Locke in America*. Lawrence, KS: University of Kansas Press.

Kramnick, Isaac. (1990), *Republicanism and Bourgeois Radicalism*. Ithaca, NY: Cornell University Press.

Lanquet, Hubert and Mornay, Philippe. (1994), *Vindiciae, Contra Tyrannos*. Edited and translated by George Garnett, Cambridge: Cambridge University Press.

Locke, John. (1823), *The Collected Works of John Locke* vol 6. London, printed for Thomas Tegg et al. (containing the four letters concerning toleration).

— (1959), *An Essay Concerning Human Understanding* (*ECHU*). A. C. Fraser (ed.) New York: Dover Publishing.

— (1960), *Two Treatises of Government* (I). Peter Laslett (ed.) Cambridge: Cambridge University Press.

— (1980), *Second Treatise of Government* (II).C. B. MacPherson (ed.) Indianapolis: Hackett Publishing.

— (1983), *A Letter Concerning Toleration*. James Tully (ed.) Indianapolis, IN: Hackett Publishing.

— (1997), *Essays on the Law of Nature*, in *Locke: Political Essays*. Mark Goldie (ed.) Cambridge: Cambridge University Press.

Lomasky, Loren. (1987), *Persons, Rights, and the Moral Community*. Oxford: Oxford University Press.

Mack, Eric. (1986), "The Ethics of Taxation: Rights versus Public Goods?" in Dwight Lee (ed.) *Taxation and the Deficit Economy*. San Francisco: Pacific Research Institute, 487–514.

— (2001), "The State of Nature Has a Law of Nature to Govern It," in Tibor Machan (ed.) *Individual Rights Reconsidered,* Stanford, CA: Hoover Institution, 87–112.

— (2002a), "Self-ownership, Marxism, and Egalitarianism: Part I," *Politics, Philosophy, and Economics* 1, 1, 75–108

— (2002b), "Self-ownership, Marxism, and Egalitarianism: Part II," *Politics, Philosophy, and Economics* 1, 2, 237–76.

Mayer, David. (1992), "The English Radical Whig Origins of American Constitutionalism," *Washington University Law Quarterly* 70, 1, 131–208.

Myers, Peter. (1998), *Our Only Star and Compass.* Lanham, MD: Rowman and Littlefield.

Nozick, Robert. (1974), *Anarchy, State and Utopia.* New York: Basic Books.

Otteson, James. (ed.) (2003), *The Levellers: Overton, Walwyn, and Lilburne.* Five volumes. Bristol: Thoemmes Press.

Parry, Geraint. (1978), *John Locke.* London: Allen and Unwin.

Penington, Jr., Isaac. (1999), "The Right, Liberty, and Safety of the People Briefly Assessed," in Joyce Lee Malcolm (ed.) *The Struggle for Sovereignty,* volume I. Indianapolis, IN: Liberty Fund, 448–89.

Peterson, Merrill D. (ed.) (1984). *Thomas Jefferson Writings.* New York: The Library of America.

Pocock, J. G. A. (1975), *The Machiavellian Moment.* Princeton: Princeton University Press.

Proast, Jonas. (1984), *The Philosophy of John Locke.* Volume 12 of the Garland Press series, Peter Schouls (ed.) New York: Garland Publishing.

Rawls, John. (1971), *A Theory of Justice.* Cambridge, MA: Harvard University Press.

Sidney, Algernon. (1990), *Discourses Concerning Government.* Thomas West (ed.) Indianapolis, IN: Liberty Classics.

Simmons, A. John. (1992), *The Lockean Theory of Rights.* Princeton: Princeton University Press.

— (1993), *On the Edge of Anarchy.* Princeton, NJ: Princeton University Press.

Schmidtz, David. (1991), *The Limits of Government.* Boulder, CO: Westview Press.

Steiner, Hillel. (1974), "The Concept of Justice," *Ratio* 16, 206–25.

Trenchard, John, and Gordon, Thomas. (1995), *Cato's Letters.* Ronald Hamowy (ed.) Indianapolis, IN: Liberty Fund, Inc.

Tuck, Richard. (1979), *Natural Right Theories.* Cambridge: Cambridge University Press.

Tucker, Robert C. (ed.) (1978), *The Marx-Engels Reader,* 2nd ed., New York: W.W. Norton.

Tully, James. (1980), *A Discourse on Property.* Cambridge: Cambridge University Press.

Tyrrell, James. (1681), *Monarcha non Patriarcha.* London: Richard Janeway. Available electronically in Early English Books Online http://eebo.chadwyck.com/search/full_rec?SOURCE=pgimages.cfg&ACTION=ByID&ID=V50833 (accessed December 14, 2008).

Vaughn, Karen. (1980), *John Locke: Economist and Social Scientist.* Chicago, IL: University of Chicago Press.

Vernon, Richard. (1997), *The Career of Toleration*. Montreal: McGill-Queen's Press.

Waldron, Jeremy. (1988), "Locke: Toleration and the Rationality of Persecution," in Susan Mendus (ed.) *Justifying Toleration*. Cambridge: Cambridge University Press, 61–86.

— (2002), *God, Locke, and Equality*. Cambridge: Cambridge University Press.

Wills, Gary. (1979), *Inventing America*. New York: Vintage Books.

Zuckert, Michael. (1994), *Natural Rights and the New Republicanism*. Princeton, NJ: Princeton University Press.

Index

Made in United States
North Haven, CT
23 January 2022

15188796R00104